SORTED

a rookie's guide to crackin' cooking

"I think it's a great idea what you're doing...
get out there and teach the young how to cook."
Ainsley Harriott

"All singing, all dancing YouTube gurus who are
intent on transforming our lives..."
The Guardian

"Ben Ebbrell and his team supply both recipes and enthusiasm
to encourage any kitchen novice to have a go.
SORTED shows that cooking can be as much fun as eating."
Mostly Food Journal

"SORTED takes the fuss out of food.
Instead, it makes good food fun, and is sure to get
tomorrow's cooks into the kitchen today."
First News, the national newspaper for young people

"Fresh look, fresh flavours, fresh approach, with a dash of
cheeky humour – it all adds up to an appealing and
much welcome new cookbook."
www.cookbookswelove.com

"Vibrant and fun – great photography, exciting recipes,
easy to follow instructions, and lively writing!"
www.notdelia.co.uk (for people who care about their food)

STAINLESS STEEL

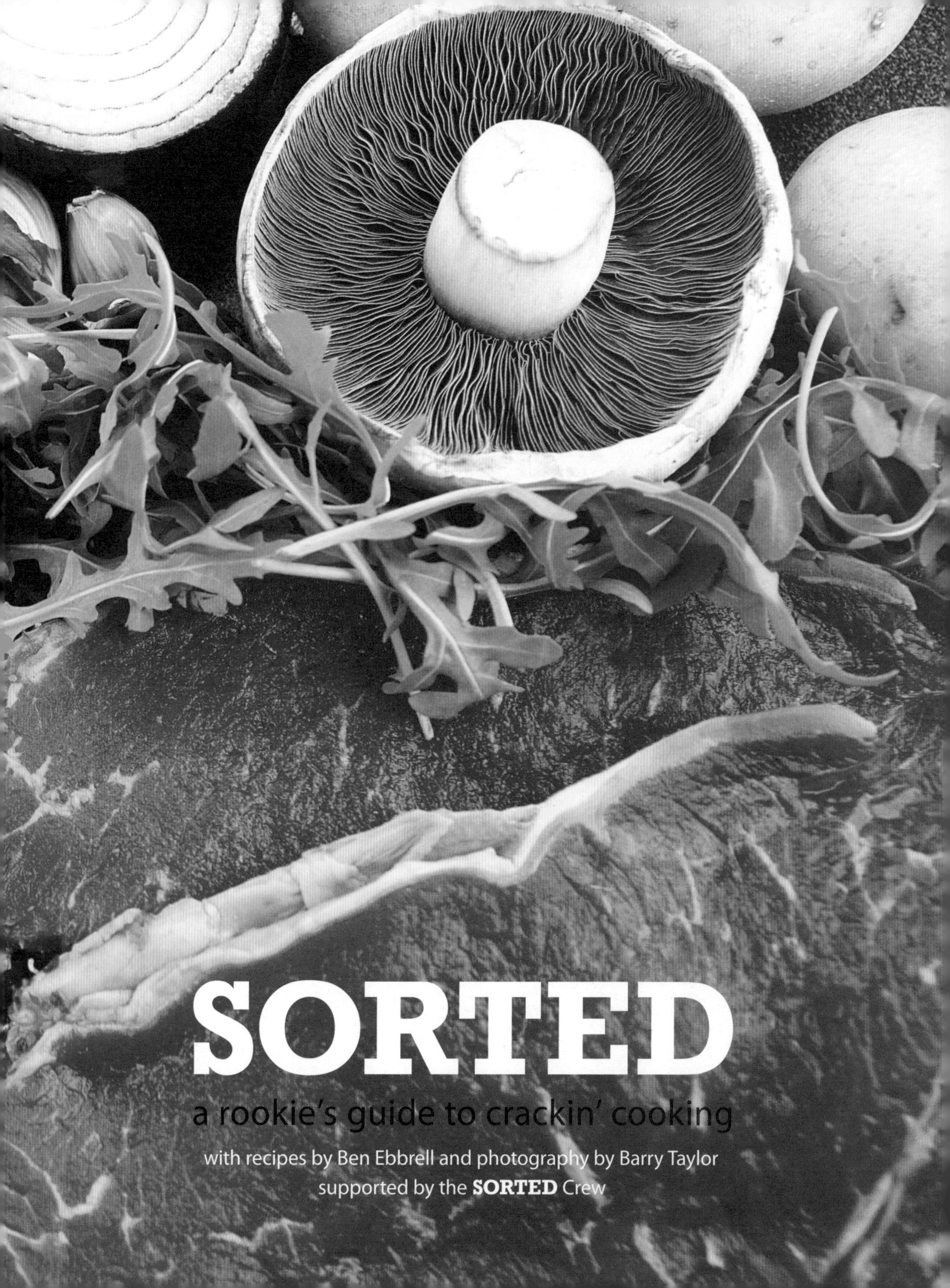

SORTED

a rookie's guide to crackin' cooking

with recipes by Ben Ebbrell and photography by Barry Taylor
supported by the **SORTED** Crew

First published in 2010 by
Co-incidence Ventures Ltd
www.co-incidence.com

SORTED

a rookie's guide to crackin' cooking

A CIP catalogue record for this book is available from the British Library.

ISBN 978-0-9559408-2-8

Edited by Wendy Toole
Artwork by Hanne Kjeldsen
Printed and bound in the UK by Maurice Payne
Colourprint Limited, RG7 4PF

Some of our recipes contain raw eggs. These recipes should be avoided by infants, pregnant women, the elderly and anyone suffering or recovering from an illness.

www.sortedfood.com

for more great recipes, videos and news, visit us online

contents

introduction

Is it time to lose your virginity in the kitchen?

SORTED helps you build the basic skills, understand fundamental cooking principles and then start to produce food to enjoy and be proud of. As your competency grows you can begin to express yourself through food, experiment with it and have FUN. We're not talking about plugging carrot sticks up your nose, flicking mashed potato across the table or laughing at every curiously shaped root vegetable – although they never cease to amaze! Simply experimenting in the kitchen, playing not only with food but developing your own skills. The possibilities are endless!

SORTED focuses on core skills and techniques to give you a solid knowledge to build on. Arm yourself with the musketeer knife skills to murder that onion, learn how to cook the ultimate steak and how to fillet a fish – it's easier than you think. Then put these skills to good use through our carefully selected recipes that enable the rookie to produce fantastic grub, begin to build confidence and to get the know-how.

While actors follow the script, builders the blueprints and newsreaders are restrained by the autocue, keen amateur cooks, accomplished amateurs and professional chefs should all have the freedom to experiment a little. A recipe is a guide only, so feel free to tweak and adapt the recipe to suit your mood and your palate. At **SORTED** we do it our way – no frills, no nonsense, no barriers – just inspired to give it a go!

To kick-off let us take you through some wet and wild soups, tailor-made jackets, mouth-watering wraps, quesadillas and sarnies. The humble lettuce leaf then strikes back with a vengeance in our salad chapter and we up the ante as we then explain how to knock up the ultimate meat and two veg! Steaks, fish, pies, bangers and mash, stew and dumplings – they're all here too. Hungry yet?

Then the devil's work hits the headlines with homemade cookies, cakes, tempting tarts and indulgent puddings galore. As if that's not enough they're all washed down with some of our shakes, non-alcoholic punches and cocktails.

Baking cakes, bread and desserts might need a little precision, but on the whole a recipe is just a guideline. So once you've got your culinary mojo the only limit is your own imagination. Brace yourself… it could be a bumpy ride! But you'll enjoy every second of it!

introducing the SORTED chef

Ben Ebbrell, 22, is a professionally trained chef (who occasionally cooks for celebs). His passion is to put the fun into cooking and help other young cooks to enjoy it every bit as much as he does.

SORTED was born when Ben, together with a bunch of his old school friends, decided to create a cookery book for students by students. The result, '**SORTED**: a recipe for student survival', was published while Ben was still in his final year at university and has proved hugely successful. This, his second book, '**SORTED**: a rookie's guide to crackin' cooking' is designed for all young novice cooks. We hope it encourages you to have a go too!

Along with the **SORTED** Crew, Ben has appeared on many national TV and radio programmes and was the winner of a national search for the next celebrity chef on the Good Food Channel's *Market Kitchen*. Ben says:

"I'm most at home when in the kitchen. I've always loved experimenting with food and understood very early on that the occasional disaster was all part of the learning process. Once I got that principle straight in my head it was quite liberating – no more fear of failure, just a real appetite for discovering what I could come up with."

"Anyone can grasp the basics of good cooking. Then the fun really starts..."

Right… let's get cracking as we delve into the wonderful and whacky world of soup. Every example in this chapter, and stacks more besides, all materialise from one insanely simple method.

Soup can be one of the quickest and easiest dishes to prepare and there are limitless varieties – there's a soup out there for everyone!

Soups are hassle-free, dirt cheap, wholesome, healthy and unbelievably tasty. And for a sense of adventure, why not experiment with some refreshing chilled soups for those scorching hot summer days? Go on, be brave!

Once you have the basic method sussed, the ingredients you choose can be manipulated again and again. This chapter explains the three key stages to creating a great soup:

1 preparing a soup base
2 making a stock
3 adding ingredients and flavour from our soup recipes

And remember, keep an eye on our website at www.sortedfood.com for more great recipes.

looks like Adam's a mug rather than a bowl person...

Ben

soup base

The key to any good soup is the base – the starting point. For every variation that **SORTED** is preparing, we begin with cooking some diced onion and crushed garlic. If you're not too handy with a knife then where better to start developing your knife skills than here? Aim for a fine and controlled dice, as demonstrated. This definitely gets easier with practice. And who cares if the first few attempts aren't that neat? The whole thing is going to be blitzed up in a blender anyway! Just take your time and be careful.

DICING AN ONION

1. Top and tail the onion.
2. Stand it up on one end and cut down onto the board, slicing the onion in half.
3. Peel away the outer layer of skin and lay each half flat with the root end furthest from the knife.
4. Make several cuts ¾ of the way into the onion towards its root.
5. Finish by slicing the onion in the opposite direction at 90 degrees to your first cuts, holding onto the root with your fingers well out of the way. When you're done you should have diced at least ¾ of the onion perfectly, leaving you with just the root. You can keep the root as it's great for stocks, stews and some soups.

PREPARING GARLIC

1. Push down on the entire garlic bulb to separate the cloves.
2. Cut into the very top of the clove.
3. Squash the clove with the side of the knife and a firm hit, keeping your fist away from the blade edge. The papery casing will now easily slide off.
4. Run the knife through the peeled and slightly smashed clove, or push through a press.

chopped onion and garlic

Each of our soup recipes in this chapter will make at least 1 litre – enough for 4 portions. They all require the same starting point of onion and garlic.

dice 1 peeled onion and fry in a saucepan (at least 2.5 litres) with a shot of olive oil for 2 minutes.

peel and **crush** 1 large clove of garlic or 2 small.

sweat this off in with the frying onions by covering the pan with a lid for 2 minutes until the onion is translucent and soft.

That's it! Your **soup base** is ready. Now head over to page 16 to make your own stock.

1
onion
2
3
4
5
1
garlic
2
3
4

making the stock

Three essential stocks are vegetable, meat (chicken or beef) and fish. Although prepared slightly differently these are fundamentally the same thing – the strained liquid from the process of simmering bones and/or meat, vegetables and seasonings. Basically, stock is the wet bit that binds our soups together!

Professional kitchens often have a stockpot simmering at all times to lob vegetable offcuts and roasted bones into. More realistically, at home you can brew up a large batch whenever it's convenient and you have the leftovers to do so, before freezing the stock down in small portions. That way there's always some knocking around when it's needed…

There's a classic combination of root vegetables that works with all stocks and a few things that definitely need avoiding! Onion, celery and carrot form the traditional starting point, often supported by leeks, garlic, mushrooms and tomatoes. Whole peppercorns, bay leaves and parsley stalks are also a good idea, but steer clear of potatoes and cabbage as these make the stock look like cloudy dishwater.

veg stock

2 onions, halved
1 head of garlic, halved
1 stick of celery
2 carrots
handful of leek tops
peppercorns (about 12)
3 bay leaves
fresh parsley stalks (the bits you don't use elsewhere!)
2–3 litres of water

wash any dirt from the vegetables you're using and chop them roughly – no need to peel!
fry them off in a very hot saucepan with a dash of oil, stopping just before they burn.
cover with plenty of water, add your herbs and spices and simmer for 1 hour.
strain through a fine sieve, chuck the vegetables away and portion out the stock before cooling.
store chilled for 3–4 days or frozen for 3–4 months.

chicken stock

halve the vegetables used for **veg stock** and include a whole chicken carcass (cooked or raw).

apply the same method as before but start by roasting the bones in a very hot oven for half an hour.

add the roasted bones to your stock pan once the vegetables are coloured and continue as before.

fish stock

halve the vegetables used for **veg stock** and include raw fish bones.

add the hacked-up fish bones and heads to the browned vegetables as for the **veg stock**.

bring to the boil and simmer for only 20 minutes before straining – leave it much longer than that and the stock will go cloudy.

Or if you'd rather discreetly cheat and use a stock cube instead, go to the individual soup recipes that begin on page 18.

soup recipes

With your soup base and stock now ready, choose the individual soup recipe you like the look of.

chilli sweetcorn soup

1 red chilli

thumb-sized chunk of fresh ginger

1 × soup base

frozen sweetcorn, thawed (750g)

chicken stock (1 litre)

2 spring onions

de-seed the chilli and dice it finely.

grate the peeled ginger and add to the prepared **soup base** with the chilli to fry for 2 minutes.

tip in the sweetcorn and cover with your **chicken stock**.

simmer for 10 minutes to soften the sweetcorn and release the flavours.

blitz in a blender, then push through a fine sieve.

season with salt and pepper and garnish with finely sliced spring onions and chilli.

roasted tomato and smoky bacon soup

16 large ripe tomatoes

6 rashers of smoked back bacon

1 × soup base

veg stock (1 litre)

fresh basil, chopped

halve the tomatoes, lay them on an oiled baking tray and roast in a hot oven at 220°C for half an hour.

slice the bacon into strips, after removing the rind.

fry the strips of bacon in with the prepared **soup base** until golden.

add the roasted tomatoes, cover with **veg stock** and simmer for about 15 minutes.

blitz in a blender, strain to remove the tomato skins and season with salt and pepper.

finish with finely shredded basil and extra grilled bacon.

spiced parsnip soup

3 or 4 parsnips (about 750g)

1 tbsp garam masala (Indian spice blend)

1 × soup base

veg stock (1 litre)

splash of double cream

    mins

peel and slice the parsnips – exact size isn't important so long as the pieces are all the same.

spoon the ground spice into a pan with the **soup base** and fry, without a lid, for 1 minute.

lob in the cut parsnips and cover with your **veg stock**.

simmer for 20 minutes, until the parsnips are tender.

blitz in a blender, season with salt and pepper and finish with cream to enrich the soup.

potato and watercress soup

1 large potato

1 × soup base

veg stock (1 litre)

big bunch of fresh watercress

    mins

peel and dice the potato into 2cm cubed pieces.

add it to the prepared **soup base** and pour in the **veg stock**.

simmer for 15 minutes, until the potatoes are cooked, then submerge the washed watercress.

bring back to the boil and cook for 1 minute.

blitz in a blender immediately to retain the vibrant green colour, season with salt and pepper and serve.

Tom
Gaz

Adam

four rookies and a saucepan,

what could go wrong?

Jamie

minty pea soup

bag of frozen peas (500g)
1 × soup base
veg stock (1 litre)
bunch of fresh mint
½ a lemon

thaw the peas.

drop the peas into a pan with the prepared **soup base** and cover with your **veg stock**.

bring to the boil, then simmer for 3 minutes.

tear the fresh mint into the soup.

blitz in a blender, strain through a sieve and season with salt and pepper.

squeeze in some lemon juice and serve.

cauliflower and toasted almond soup

¾ of a head of cauliflower
1 × soup base
veg stock (1 litre)
generous handful of almond flakes

cut the cauliflower into florets and dice up the stalk as well. Waste nothing!

add to the **soup base** and cover with the **veg stock**.

simmer for 20 minutes, until the cauliflower is tender, especially the stalks.

toast the almond flakes by tossing them in a hot, dry pan until golden, then add to the soup.

blitz in a blender, season with salt and pepper and check for personal preference – you may want a few extra almonds as their flavour can be quite subtle.

fennel and orange soup

2 bulbs of fennel
1 × soup base
veg stock (½ litre)
milk (½ litre)
1 orange

save the fennel fronds (feathery leafy bits at the top) as a decorative garnish before you slice the vegetable.

wash the cut fennel and add to the **soup base** then cover with the **veg stock** and milk.

simmer for 20 minutes to release the full flavours.

zest the orange and add to the cooked soup.

blitz in a blender, season with salt and pepper, then garnish with the fennel fronds you saved earlier.

AND IT DOESN'T STOP THERE!

If some of these suggestions have whetted your appetite, then check out our website for more great recipes at www.sortedfood.com

chilled soups

Soups don't have to be steaming hot and rationed to the winter months. Here are two suggestions that follow the same basic principles as before, except they are then chilled and sipped as a refreshing light summer soup.

chilled chilli melon soup

2 ripe cantaloupe melons
1 red chilli
1 × soup base
veg stock (1 litre)
5 spring onions

   mins + cooling

scoop the seeds out of the peeled melons and dice up the juicy flesh.

de-seed the chilli, dice it and fry it off along with the prepared **soup base**.

pour in the **veg stock** and add the melon and chopped spring onions.

simmer for just 5 minutes.

blitz in a blender until smooth.

chill well before serving with ice.

chilled cucumber soup

2–3 cucumbers
1 × soup base
1 tbsp cornflour
chicken stock (1 litre)
3 sprigs of dill
1 dollop of sour cream

   mins + cooling

peel and dice the cucumbers and add to the prepared **soup base** in a large pan.

stir the cornflour with a dash of **chicken stock** to form a lump-free paste and add to pan with the rest of the stock.

simmer for 15 minutes then blitz the soup in a blender and chill.

chop the dill as finely as possible and add to chilled soup.

whisk in the sour cream and season to taste with salt and pepper – use celery salt if you have any.

You know the feeling – you walk into a sandwich shop and you become paralysed by the amount of choice available so you bottle it and stick to what you know, quietly regretting another missed opportunity to step outside your comfort zone.

This chapter will help you to make a range of delicious toppings and fillings, with ideas for wraps, quesadillas, slammin' sandwiches and jacket potatoes.

Sandwiches can be truly epic with a little bit of imagination (and great bread) and jacket potatoes can be so much more than just... well... jacket potatoes!

We'll run through our tips for preparing the ultimate jacket, how to make your own bread (it's not that scary) and a few ideas on top toasties.

And remember, keep an eye on our website at www.sortedfood.com for more great recipes.

Barry

SORTED

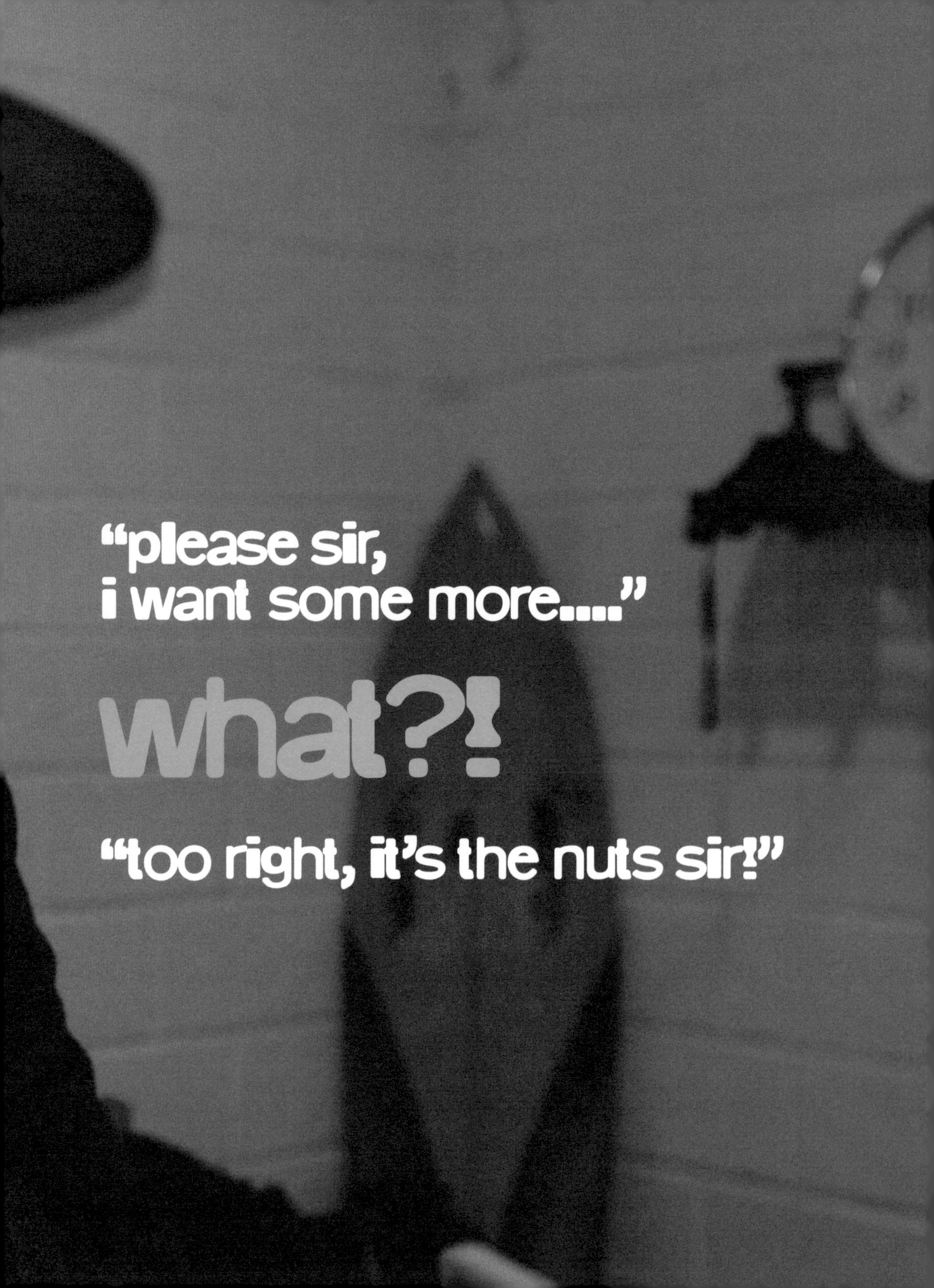

"please sir,
i want some more...."

what?!

"too right, it's the nuts sir!"

the ultimate jacket

Nothing beats a hot, fluffy jacket potato with crispy skin, served with a generous dollop of chilli con carne and grated cheese on Bonfire Night. And that's what we've got here – but remember remember, it's not just limited to the fifth of November. Nor just chilli. Here's how to make the best comfort food going!

A WINNING RESULT

1. The best potatoes to use are the white, floury, non-waxy ones – like Maris Piper or King Edward.
2. Shape and size really does matter! Go for a round potato rather than an elongated flat one and aim for something around 400g in weight.
3. Preheat the oven to 190°C. Scrub the potatoes clean, then prick them all over with a fork to stop the skins bursting as they cook.
4. Season some olive oil and use it to rub over the pricked skins.
5. Bung the potatoes onto the middle shelf of the hot oven for 1½–2 hours, turning over half way through.

CUTTING CORNERS

Of course, if you can't handle the hunger pains long enough to bake a potato the traditional way, then preheat the oven to 220°C while you run through points 1, 2 and 3. Then nuke the spud in the microwave on full power for 8–10 minutes. Now rub in seasoned oil and crisp up in the preheated oven for at least 20 minutes, until you just can't survive the wait any longer!

FANCY A TOPPING OR A FILLING?

The same thing? Oh no. We reckon that if you scoop out the cooked flesh, mix it with your ingredients and refill the skins then it's a filling. A dollop of something slopped over the cut potato would be a topping! Simple! The following pages include some popular options.

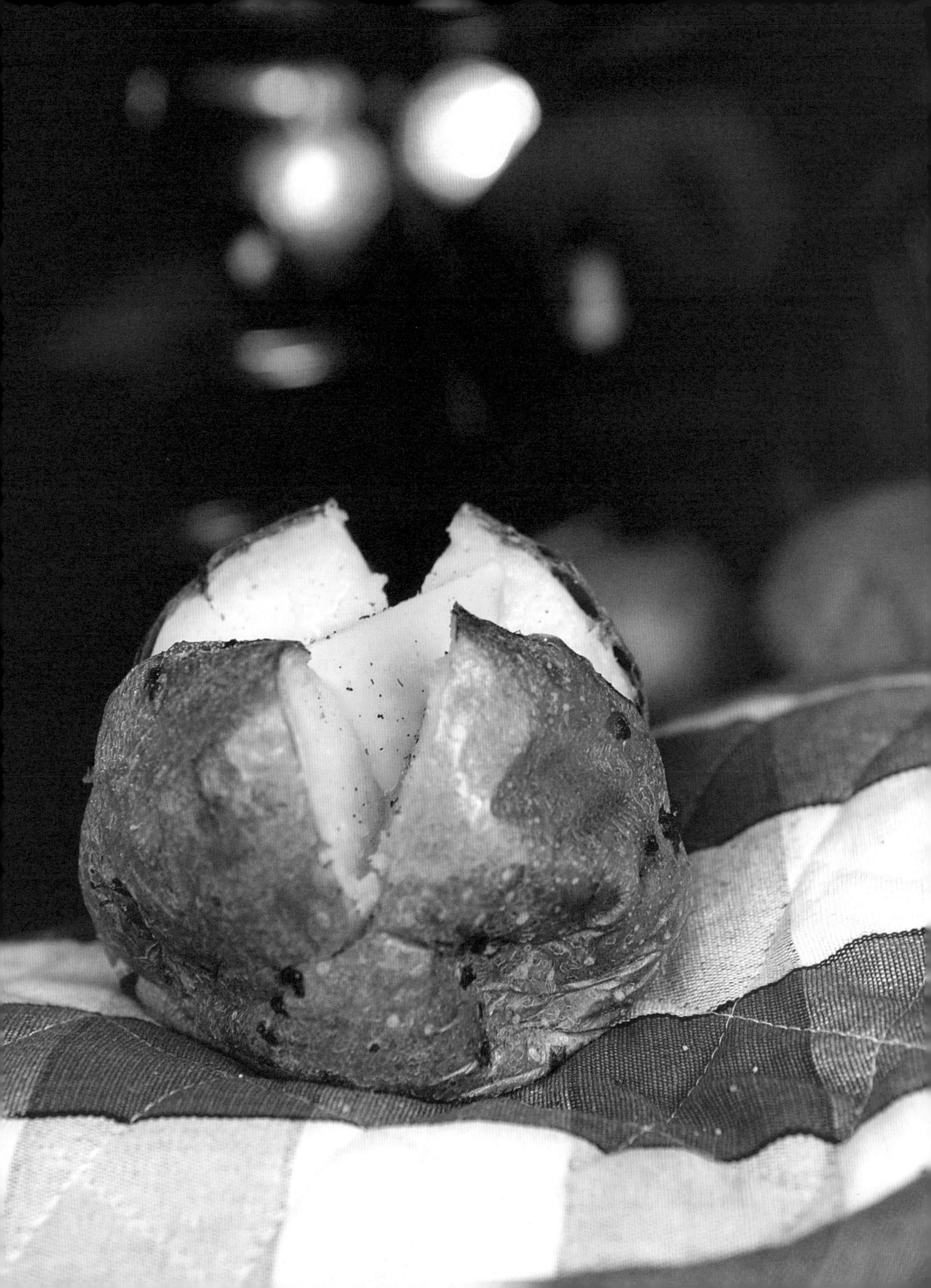

chilli con carne topping

- 1 large onion
- 2 cloves of garlic
- 1 red chilli
- olive oil
- 1 green pepper
- 1 tsp chilli powder
- 1 tsp ground cinnamon
- 1 tsp ground cumin
- beef mince (500g)
- large glass of red wine
- tin of chopped tomatoes (400g)
- cup of water
- squeeze of tomato purée
- tin of kidney beans (400g)
- 4 × ultimate jackets

peel and dice the onion and garlic and chop up the chilli, keeping the seeds in.

fry them all in a large deep pan with a shot of olive oil.

de-seed the green pepper and add this to the cooking onions.

spoon in the spices and mix, then add the minced beef.

fry for 3–4 minutes before you slosh in the red wine.

tip in the tomatoes, water and a squeeze of tomato purée.

bubble the mixture for at least an hour before adding the drained kidney beans.

simmer for a further hour, then season with salt and pepper and serve over **ultimate jackets**, topped with grated cheese, sour cream or guacamole.

store any leftovers in the fridge – it tastes even better the next day!

prawn and spring onion filling

handful of frozen cooked prawns

couple of spring onions

1 × ultimate jacket

few sprigs of fresh parsley

1 tbsp mayonnaise

sprinkle of paprika

butter

mins

thaw the prawns and squeeze out any excessive liquid.

chop the spring onions and parsley as finely as possible.

scoop the cooked flesh (that's the potato bit in the potato) from the halved **ultimate jacket** while it's still hot and place in a bowl. Keep the skins for later.

mix the prawns, mayo, onions, parsley and paprika into the potato flesh.

season with salt and pepper then re-fill the skins.

dot the top of the potato with a couple of tiny knobs of butter, then return to the hot oven for 10 minutes to go golden brown.

serve immediately with a crisp salad.

creamy brie mushroom filling

½ an onion

olive oil

1 clove of garlic

large handful of button mushrooms

double cream (about 50ml)

black pepper

couple of fresh chives

wedge of brie cheese

1 × ultimate jacket

mins

dice the onion as finely as you can and fry in a pan with a dash of oil for 2 minutes.

crush the garlic, add to the pan and fry for another minute.

halve the mushrooms and pan fry until soft.

pour in the cream, then add some black pepper and the finely sliced chives.

break over the brie and heat it until it all melts.

scoop the cooked flesh from the halved **ultimate jacket** potato while still hot and place in a bowl.

add the brie-mushroom mixture, stir through and then re-fill the potato skins.

return to the oven to colour the top and serve immediately with a crisp salad.

Ben

Lora

woo the ladies with your
SORTED snacks and see what
they fancy for afters...

Jamie

wraps

chicken caesar

handful of crisp lettuce leaves – little gem or cos varieties are perfect

½ a cooked chicken breast, sliced

2 anchovies

spoonful of caesar dressing

sprinkling of parmesan shavings

tear the lettuce leaves into pieces.

mix all the ingredients together in a bowl.

pile the filling into your tortilla wrap and enjoy.

duck and plum sauce

few spring onions

¼ of a cucumber

shredded duck meat

1 tsp plum sauce or hoisin sauce

slice the spring onions across finely and cut the cucumber into matchstick-sized pieces.

arrange on the wrap.

mix together the duck and the plum sauce and spoon onto the wrap before folding.

chilli crab

tin of white crab meat (170g)

1 lime

½ a red chilli

sprig of fresh coriander

dollop of mayonnaise to bind

crisp lettuce

couple of slices of tomato

drain the crab meat and place in a bowl.

zest the lime into the bowl.

dice and de-seed the chilli and chop the coriander.

combine with the mayo and crab meat in the bowl, season well with salt and pepper, then serve in a wrap with lettuce and tomato.

£   mins

quesadillas

Using the wraps in a different way, these great little Spanish tapas snacks make a really quick and simple casing for just about any filling you like. They usually contain a mixture of chicken, cheese and chilli but we think that anything that works on a pizza will be great in a quesadilla. Just pick your ideal pizza topping from the takeaway menu and rustle up your own version for a fraction of the price. Here are our favourites...

lay out a tortilla and sprinkle with a handful of grated cheese, either cheddar or mozzarella.

scatter your additional chosen filling over and finish with more cheese.

whack another tortilla on top and fry in medium pan with a spot of oil, turning once, until crisp.

quarter into portions and serve with your preferred dip.

sweet potato and blue cheese

small sweet potato

chunk of blue cheese

½ a red onion

peel the sweet potato and dice into 1cm pieces.

place in a pan of salted cold water.

bring to the boil and simmer for about 8 minutes, until the potato is cooked through.

drain the potato and leave to cool.

crumble the blue cheese and finely slice the onion.

red onion marmalade and goat's cheese

3 red onions

shot of oil

brown sugar (50g)

balsamic vinegar (50ml)

glass of red wine (150ml)

goat's cheese (100g)

fresh basil

peel and slice the red onions, then fry in a pan with the hot oil for 5 minutes, until softened.

sprinkle in the brown sugar, then add the vinegar and wine.

simmer for 15 minutes, until the onions have a syrupy consistency. Then cool.

crumble the goat's cheese into a bowl.

pick a handful of fresh basil leaves.

££ ×2 mins

ham, mushroom and tarragon

2 or 3 field mushrooms
butter
few slices of cooked ham
sprig of fresh tarragon

slice the mushrooms and fry in a hot pan with a knob of butter so they go a golden colour.

season well with salt and pepper.

cut up the ham.

pluck the leaves from the tarragon stalks and chop finely.

heavenly bread

Baking bread is the chef's answer to a stress ball. The process of mixing and kneading can be really therapeutic, and if nothing else the aroma of freshly baked bread is second to none. So next time you're hungry for a fight, let off some steam and show the dough what you're made of. It does take a little precision and care, but with the right technique making bread isn't out of reach of anyone, novice or not. The main ingredients of flour, yeast and water are dirt cheap and the results are simply gorgeous.

TRADITIONAL DOUGH

strong bread flour (1kg)
2 tbsp sugar
1 tbsp salt
dried fast action yeast (3 × 7g sachets)
warm water (600ml)

1. Sift the flour into a bowl and pour in the sugar and salt. Stir.
2. Mix the yeast with a dash or two of the warm water to form a smooth liquid.
3. Add the yeast mixture to the flour, then add the remaining water a little at a time.
4. Stir until it comes together to form one dough ball. You may not need all the water.
5. Massage the dough continuously for at least 5 minutes on a clean work surface until it's silky, soft and elastic. This is called kneading!
6. Dust the top of the dough with a little extra flour, put it in a clean bowl and cover with cling film. Leave the dough in a warm place for about 40 minutes to let the yeast work its magic and for the dough to double in size. This is the all-important 'proving' stage.
7. Knock the air out of the dough by kneading it for 30 seconds and add any flavouring that you wish. Grated cheese, toasted cumin seeds or chopped olives are some of our favourites.
8. Shape the dough ready for baking, place it on a baking tray and allow to prove for at least another 30 minutes to double in size again. Preheat the oven to 180°C in the meantime. Place the dough in the oven carefully so as not to knock the air back out of it again and bake until it's golden and the bread sounds hollow when tapped from underneath. This will take about 40 minutes for a single loaf.
9. Remove from the oven and transfer to a wire rack to cool. Slice and enjoy when cooled.

2.5 hrs | makes 1 loaf

When you've tried a SORTED recipe, tell us about it at www.sortedfood.com

1
2
3
4
5
6
7
8
9

slammin' sandwiches

A packed lunch doesn't have to be a sandwich, but if it is then make sure it's homemade! Of course, we don't always have time to bake our own bread – but try to at least find time to make your own sarnies as the ones you buy from shops can be expensive, high in salt and brimming with saturated fats. And while you're at it, you can make it just the way you like it. For a little inspiration, here are some of our favourite sandwich fillings.

mango chicken

cooked chicken breast

dollop of mayonnaise

1 tbsp mango chutney

handful of fresh coriander

dice the chicken into pieces and dump into a bowl.

spoon in equal quantities of mayo and chutney, season with salt and pepper and mix together.

tear up the coriander leaves and mix these through too.

fill your sandwich with plenty of the mixture.

avocado and bacon

3 rashers of smoked bacon

1 ripe avocado

¼ of a red onion

1 tsp mayonnaise

grill the bacon on a wire rack until golden and crispy.

halve the avocado, remove the stone and scoop out the flesh.

slice the avocado and onion fairly finely and mix in a bowl with the mayo.

spoon the filling onto the bacon, wedged between two thick slices of brown bread.

SORTED spiced tomato chutney

If you fancy going the extra mile and making your own chutney, here's how...

1 clove of garlic
1 red onion
1 red eating apple
ripe tomatoes (500g)
small handful of sultanas
1 tsp grated fresh ginger
1 tsp mustard seeds
pinch of ground cloves
brown sugar (100g)
malt vinegar (250ml)

grate the garlic.

peel and dice the red onion and apple.

chop up the tomatoes.

put all the fruit, vegetables and dry ingredients into a deep pan with half the vinegar.

bring to a simmer and cook for 45 minutes.

add the remaining vinegar and cook for a further 30 minutes, until the mixture is a syrupy consistency.

pour into a clean jam jar and cool.

store in the fridge for up to 3 months, using it alongside cooked meats and cheese in sandwiches.

hrs | makes 1 jar

top toasties

A brilliant little sandwich toastie machine can help you to create a shed-load of warm, comforting snacks that hold just about anything you like. So quick to use and requiring nothing more than a quick wipe down afterwards, the toastie machine is a little godsend.

Simply butter two slices of bread on one side. Lay one slice butter side down on the preheated cast-iron plate and arrange your filling on top. Complete with the other slice of bread (butter side up) then carefully close the lid, set the timer for 4 minutes... and it's job done! That's right... think of it as an inside-out sarnie, with the buttered bread facing outward.

cheese and mushroom

The oils released from the cheese will cook the mushrooms perfectly in the 4 minutes.

2 mushrooms

cheddar cheese (50g)

2 spring onions

wash the mushrooms and slice them as finely as possible.

slice the cheese so you have enough to cover the base of the toastie.

chop the spring onions.

lay the cheese onto the bread, top with mushrooms and then finish with onion.

each (£) (☺) (×1) (◷) mins

ham and egg

Sounds risky but this works a treat. Once you've cracked it, you'll be hooked!

1 egg

couple of slices of cooked ham

push the base layer of bread down into the grooves of the toastie machine.

crack the egg into this well, moving the yolk to one side and the majority of the white to the other.

lay the ham slices over the egg, taking care not to break the yolk, and cover with the second slice of bread.

cook for 4–5 minutes to create a perfectly baked egg held within the bread. Best served with brown sauce.

sweet

banana and peanut butter

You're not restricted to savoury toasties. Bread works well in numerous puddings and this is no exception. Try this sweet little number and you won't look back.

1 small banana

1 tbsp crunchy peanut butter

slice the banana quite thinly and arrange on the bread.

spread the peanut butter across the toastie and top with the bread lid.

cook as normal and enjoy for dessert with a scoop of vanilla ice cream.

You don't need to be a ravenous rabbit after a long day's 'loving' to appreciate a good salad.

We are delighted to present here some of the SORTED Crew's favourite salad ideas.

These salads are all able to successfully hold their own on the barbecue spread, claiming their rightful place alongside the ever so slightly overdone sausage or chicken skewer and the monster-burger. Or for lunch they can be the subject of true envy as you nonchalantly whip out a tub of your own salad creation to trump the supermarket alternatives of your friends.

Once you've got the foundations of the salad, whether that's pasta, potato, couscous or beans, the rest is up to you. Dress it in vinaigrette, flavoured mayonnaise or pesto and bulk it out with anything vibrant and fresh. We're aiming for colour, flavour and texture here to ensure these salads are the business.

Any rabbit that gets hold of one of these salads will be as lucky as... well... his own back foot!

(rabbit food)

if it's good enough for Thumper, it's good enough for me

salad foundations

COOKING DRIED PASTA

1. For a main-course portion allow 100g of pasta per person, or about 50g per person for a salad. Aim for about a litre of salted water in the pan per 100g of pasta.
2. Only add the pasta once the water is boiling rapidly and then stir for 30 seconds to make sure the pasta doesn't stick to itself or to the pan. A rapid boil is important throughout.
   Set the timer for a minute less than it states on the packet, then test the pasta by trying a piece.
3. Drain into a colander and run under cold water to cool immediately if using for a salad, or immediately toss into your chosen sauce if serving hot.

BOILING POTATOES

1. Make sure all the potatoes are scrubbed or peeled and cut into the same-sized pieces to allow even cooking.
2. Place in a pan and cover with cold water plus a pinch of salt.
   Bring to the boil and gently simmer for 15–20 minutes for regular potatoes or 12–15 minutes for small new potatoes.
   Potatoes are ready when a sharp knife glides into the centre without resistance but the potato still holds its shape.
3. Drain in a colander and stop the cooking process quickly under cold running water.

COOKING COUSCOUS

1. Allow 50g of couscous per serving.
2. Place the required amount of couscous in a bowl and cover with an equal volume of boiling water or stock (see page 16).
   Stir to ensure that all the grains are submerged then cover the bowl with a lid, plate or cling film.
3. Leave to stand for 3–4 minutes.
   Fluff up the couscous with a fork and add the required flavourings.

1
2
3
pasta
1
2
3
potatoes
1
2
3
couscous

pasta salads

olive, caper, anchovy and basil

bowl of cooked and cooled pasta shapes
drizzle of extra virgin olive oil
2 spoonfuls of capers
handful of stoned black olives
anchovy fillets (about 6)
bunch of fresh basil
chunk of parmesan

mins

lubricate the pasta with the oil in a large bowl, to stop all the pieces bunching together.
drain the capers and the olives.
chop up the anchovy fillets and halve the olives.
tear the basil and stir the leaves through the pasta with the capers, olives and anchovies.
grate over the parmesan and combine everything.
season with pepper, avoiding salt because of the anchovies, and enjoy. Allowing the flavours to infuse for an hour or so at room temperature before eating improves this salad no end.

ham, broad bean, chive and sour cream

bowl of frozen broad beans
cooked ham
bunch of fresh chives
cooked and cooled pasta shapes
dollop of sour cream

mins

thaw the beans at room temperature.
slice the ham into slivers and snip the chives, then stir them into the pasta.
pop the beans out of their tough skins, leaving just the succulent, vibrant beans.
add to the pasta with enough sour cream to just bind.
season well with salt and pepper.

potato salads

cherry tomato and rocket

peeled and quartered potatoes (1kg)
vinaigrette (French dressing)
big handful of fresh rocket
cherry tomatoes (about 250g)
red onion

mins

boil the potatoes and drain when cooked.

shake the dressing well and drizzle over the warm potatoes. They will absorb the flavour as they cool.

rip up the rocket and halve the tomatoes.

slice the red onion as finely as possible.

mix all the ingredients together when the potatoes are cold, then season with salt and pepper and serve.

beetroot, horseradish and watercress

cooked new potatoes, skin on (1kg)
cooked beetroot – not the kind in vinegar (250g)
bunch of watercress
2 dollops of mayonnaise
spoonful of hot horseradish sauce

mins

chill the potatoes down when cooked and cut them into bite-sized pieces.

dice the beetroot and stir into the potato.

wash and roughly chop the watercress, stalks included, then add to the salad.

combine the mayo with the horseradish. The ratios depend on personal preference but remember the dressing will mellow down when added to the potato. Twice as much mayo as horseradish is a safe start.

season the salad with salt and pepper and bind it all together with the mayo.

taste and adjust horseradish and salt levels before serving.

couscous salads

spinach, pine nut and lemon

couple of fistfuls of fresh spinach

1 cup of couscous (cooked in veg stock, if possible)

handful of pine nuts

1 lemon

black pepper

bunch of fresh parsley

wash the spinach to free it from grit and add it to the couscous as it is cooking so that the spinach begins to wilt.

toast the pine nuts in a dry pan to give them a golden colour.

squeeze the lemon into the couscous bowl with a generous amount of black pepper.

chop the parsley finely and stir through the salad with the toasted pine nuts.

chorizo, feta and spring onion

chunk of chorizo

1 cup of cooked couscous (cooked in chicken stock, if possible)

slab of feta cheese

few spring onions

remove the papery skin of the chorizo and hack the sausage into small bite-sized chunks.

fry them off in a dry pan for a couple of minutes to release loads of tasty spicy oils.

stir the sausage and all of its oil into the cooked and fluffy couscous to infuse flavour and impart colour.

crumble the feta and finely slice the spring onions.

mix everything together, loosening with a little extra oil if necessary, and season well with salt and pepper.

armed and ready for lunch,
the Crew go off road
for a picnic!
LAND ROVER
HVS
406

other salads

three bean salad

tin of kidney beans (400g)
tin of butter beans (400g)
fistful of fresh French beans
bunch of spring onions
1 clove of garlic
drizzle of vinaigrette

open the tins, drain the beans in a colander and rinse under cold running water.

fill a pan with salted water and bring to the boil.

snip the tops and tails off the French beans, finely slice the spring onions and grate the garlic.

cook the French beans in the rapidly boiling water for 2–3 minutes, then drain them under cold running water to cool immediately. They should still have a 'bite' to them.

cut the cooled beans into pieces similar in size to the kidney beans and combine all the ingredients in a bowl.

season well with salt and pepper and serve.

mins

apple and celeriac coleslaw

1 celeriac

3 red eating apples

1 red onion

2 sprigs of fresh dill

2 tbsp mayonnaise

dollop of wholegrain mustard

1 lemon

cut away the tough outer layer from the celeriac and coarsely grate the vegetable.

wash and core the apples, peel the onion and grate both.

chop the fresh dill finely, then combine all the prepared ingredients in a bowl with the mayo and enough mustard for personal taste.

season with a squeeze of lemon juice and plenty of salt and pepper.

£ ×4 mins

asian bean sprout salad

½ a cucumber

handful of radishes

plenty of fresh bean sprouts

knob of fresh ginger

1 tbsp sesame oil

2 tbsp caster sugar

2 tbsp soy sauce

1 fresh red chilli

1 tbsp lime juice

wash the cucumber, halve it lengthways and scoop out the seeds and centre flesh (chuck these out as they will make the salad soggy).

slice the radishes finely and cut the cucumber into matchsticks to resemble the bean sprouts.

grate the ginger into a large bowl and mix in the oil, sugar and soy sauce.

remove the seeds from the chilli and cut it up as finely as possible. Add to the dressing.

squeeze in the lime juice, stir, then toss in all the prepared ingredients.

£ ×2 mins

Need a little more substance than just a light bite? Where better to begin than with the classic collision of meat and two veg?

And, as ever, we give it a SORTED twist to bring it bang up to date.

We've put together a collection of tasty meals that don't take any longer than peeling, chopping and boiling up a few potatoes. As usual we're taking a simple concept – mashed potato – and seeing what we can do to transform the humble spud into spud-tacular results!

Not only does the meat and mash formula provide you with a nutritionally balanced meal, but by bulking out your plate with simple ingredients like potatoes you can stretch a limited budget. The challenge is to make sure you never get fed up with the same old mash, and that's where we hope to inspire.

We'll also try to make you a dab hand with steaks – impressing like a pro when asking your guests how they'd like it cooked. In the past 'edible' may have been good enough, but now we're rocking! As if that's not enough, we pay a swift visit to our fishy friends too... demonstrating how best to fillet the slippery critters.

And remember, keep an eye on our website at www.sortedfood.com for more great recipes.

Beth, Rach and Nic experiment
with meat and two veg

classic mash

Mashed potato is mouth-watering just as it is, or can be flavoured to provide some variety. Here's how to make **classic mash** and we spice it up a little in the recipes that follow in this chapter.

potatoes (1kg) – russet or maris piper are brilliant

1 tsp salt

mug of milk

golf ball sized knob of butter

peel the spuds and quarter or halve them depending on their size – just make sure they're all roughly equal.

dump them into a pan and just cover with cold salted water.

bring to the boil and simmer for 20 minutes or so until cooked through.

poke with a skewer. There should be no resistance in the centre of the potatoes – if there is you'll end up with lumpy mash.

drain and return to the dry hot pan.

splash in the milk and butter and mash well until smooth. Simple!

£ ☺ ×4 mins

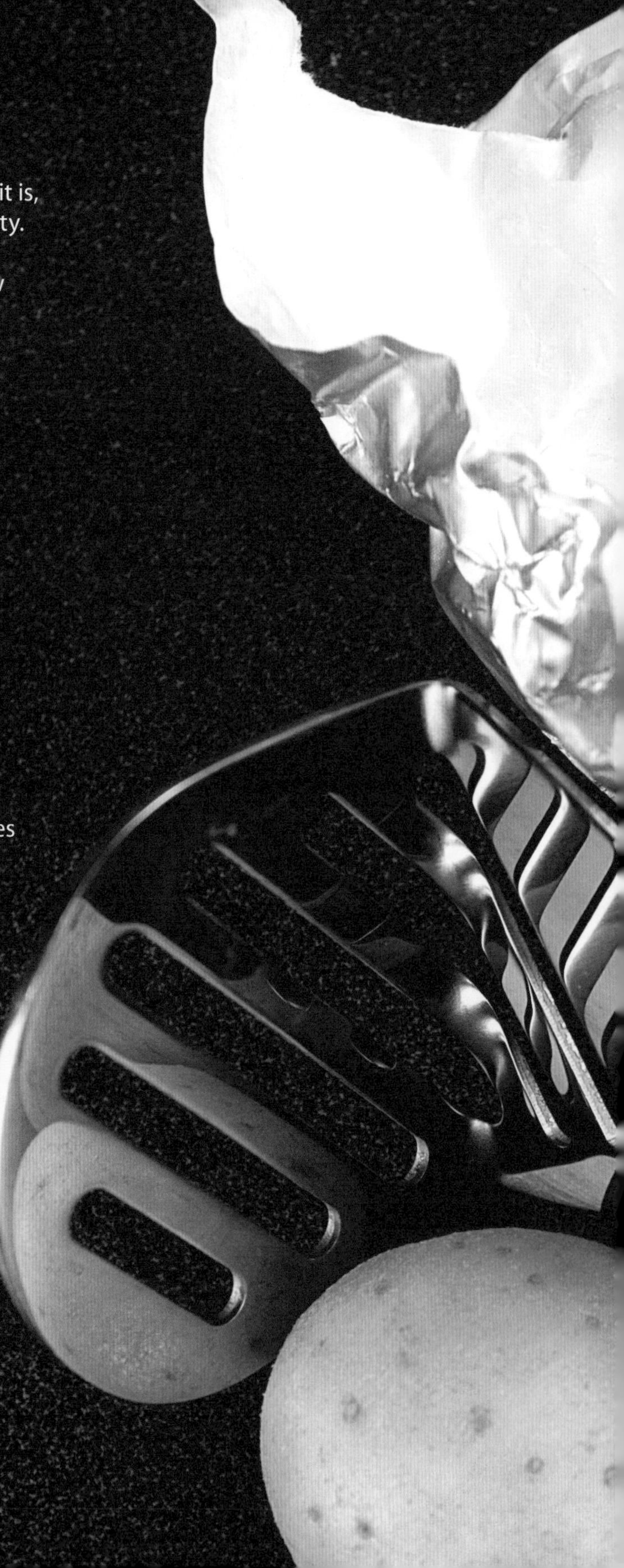

bangers and mustard mash

quality meaty sausages (about 12)
beef stock (1 litre)
1 tbsp worcestershire sauce
1 tbsp cornflour
bag of frozen peas (400g)
1 heaped tbsp wholegrain mustard
1 × classic mash
crispy onion rings (see below)

preheat the grill to a medium heat, approx 200°C.

prick the sausages and stick them on a rack under the grill for 15 minutes, turning occasionally, until golden and cooked through.

put on a pan of salted water and bring to the boil ready for the peas.

heat up the stock in another pan and whisk in the worcestershire sauce.

dissolve the cornflour in a small pot of cold water and pour into the hot stock, stirring continuously. Simmer for a few minutes to thicken.

tip the peas into the boiling water and simmer until floating – about 2–3 minutes.

beat the mustard into the hot **classic mash**.

drain the peas and serve the meal as a mountain of food to demolish with mates.

homemade onion rings

2 large white onions
beer (175ml)
plain flour (150g)
pinch of salt
veg oil for deep-frying

heat up the oil in a saucepan, taking care to only half-fill. (Never leave this unattended and if the oil begins to shimmer or smoke remove from the heat immediately.)

peel the onions and slice across to create chunky slices. Separate into individual onion rings.

whisk the beer into the flour until lump free, adding a pinch of salt.

dust the onion rings in a little extra flour and dunk into the batter.

lower carefully into the hot oil and fry for 3–4 minutes, until golden.

scoop the rings out of the oil with a fork, drain them on kitchen paper to remove excess oil and sprinkle with a little salt.

pork chop with apple and sage mash, cider cream sauce and broccoli

four hefty pork chops

1 onion

2 cloves of garlic

½ a can of cider (250ml)

head of broccoli

double cream (100ml)

1 tbsp apple sauce

few sprigs of fresh sage, finely chopped

1 × classic mash

   **mins**

preheat the grill to a medium heat.

stick a pan of salted water on and bring to the boil.

rub the chops in seasoned oil and place them under a hot grill for about 5–6 minutes on each side.

dice the onion as finely as possible, crush the garlic and fry with the lid on, in a dash of oil until soft.

crank up the heat and pour in the cider. Let it sizzle and bubble to reduce to a syrupy consistency.

prepare the broccoli by cutting it into mini florets, all roughly the same size.

pour the cream into the sauce and bring to a gentle simmer.

dump the broccoli into the rapidly boiling water and cook for about 3 minutes. The florets should still be vibrant green and have a slight 'bite' when done.

beat the apple sauce and sage through the hot **classic mash**. When the pork is cooked, serve with drained broccoli, sage mash and a drizzle of cider cream sauce.

gammon steak, tarragon mash and sautéed mushrooms

4 big field mushrooms
olive oil
knob of butter
1 clove of garlic
4 gammon steaks
handful of fresh tarragon, finely chopped
1 × classic mash

mins

scrub any dirt from the mushrooms and hack into thumb-sized pieces, stalks and all.

heat a pan for a minute or so with a shot of oil, then throw in the butter and mushrooms. Avoid moving the mushrooms too much as they cook – it's best to get golden colour on them before shaking them about and releasing too much liquid.

crush the garlic into the mushrooms halfway through cooking.

fry the gammon steaks in a pan for a couple of minutes on each side.

season the mushrooms when cooked with salt and black pepper.

beat the tarragon through the cooked **classic mash** and serve with the mushrooms and chunky gammon steak.

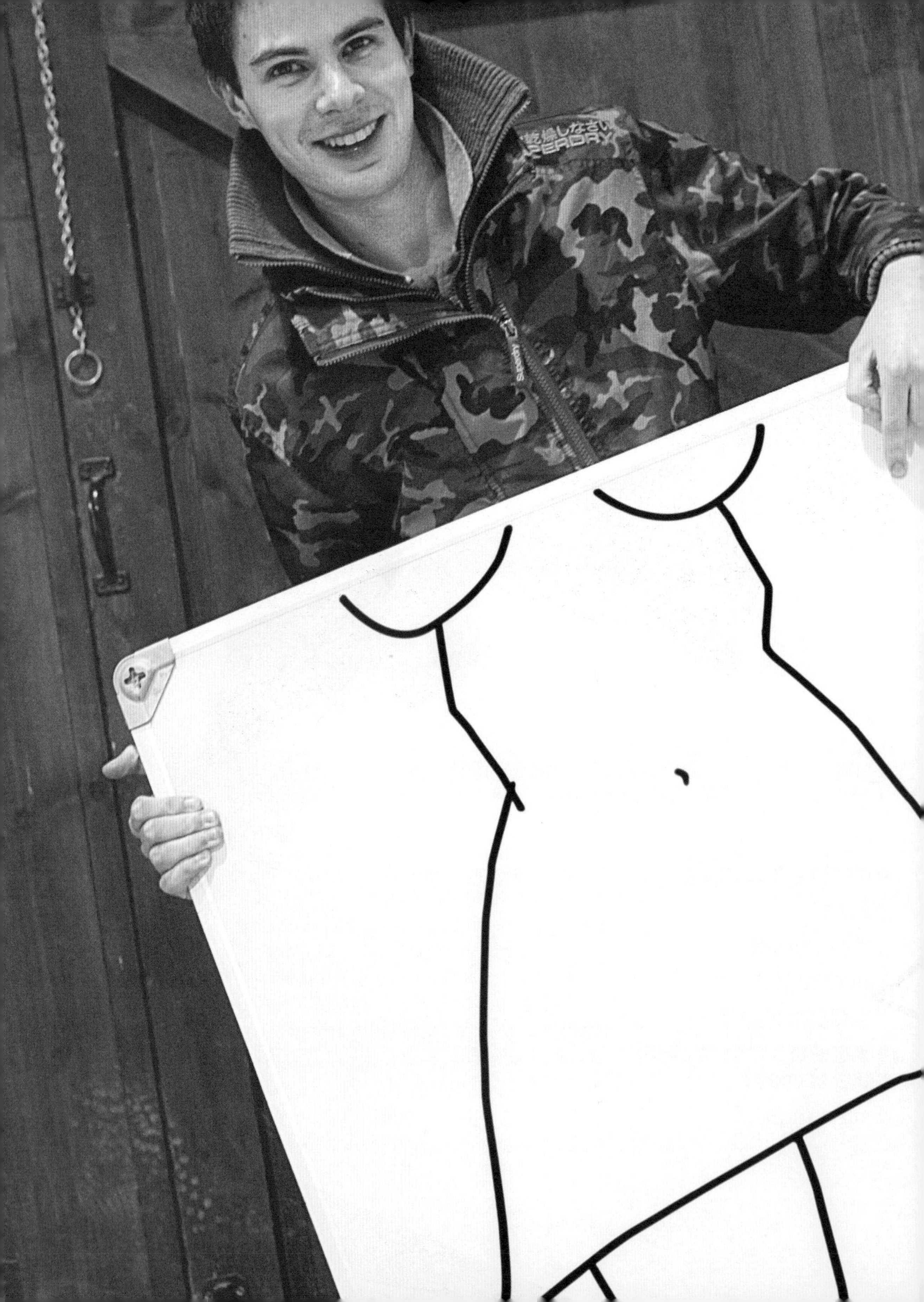

cooking is all about
confidence and fun
so serve with a smile!

pure carnivore

OIL YOUR MEAT

Forget about frying your steak as it swims about in gallons of oil! It's best to oil the meat itself. Season a small plate of oil with plenty of salt and pepper and rub this onto the steak just before adding it to the hot pan or grill.

HOT HOT HOT!

A hot pan is crucial. You want to sear the steak and seal in all that flavour. Anything less and it'll begin to stew in its own juices and you won't get that gorgeous caramelised flavour on the outside of the steak.

A BIT OF FAT WON'T HARM!

Fat isn't a bad thing in moderation – it keeps a healthy animal warm. But if the steak has a thick layer of fat on one side (like with a sirloin) then make sure it's well cooked. Stand the meat up on the fatty side in the pan because the crisp golden fat is much nicer and more presentable than the unbearable, anaemic and chewy alternative.

HOW WOULD YOU LIKE IT COOKED, SIR?

An approximate guide to cooking temperatures can be gained from the fleshy muscle in your palm at the base of your thumb. When the firmness of the steak resembles this muscle then it's at the 'rare' stage. Touch the tip of your thumb with your middle finger and now the same muscle resembles a steak cooked to 'medium'. Repeat the process again with the thumb touching the little finger and it'll be spot on for a 'well done' steak. See the demo on our website.

Time out...

When the steak's cooked how you like it, be sure to let it rest on a warm plate for 2–3 minutes. The temperature inside has to stabilise so that any remaining blood doesn't ooze out as soon as you cut through it.

CLEAR RUNNING JUICES

Chicken must always be cooked until there is no pink flesh remaining and all the juices running out of the meat are clear. Any signs of blood and it needs a little more cooking.

SECRET TO SUCCULENT CHICKEN

If you're roasting chicken on a tray then adding a little swig of water in the bottom helps to keep the meat moist and succulent, but still allows for a crispy golden skin if there is one.

GET IT RIGHT!

Pork, like chicken, is traditionally cooked right through. Take care not to overcook pork though as it can go very dry and rubbery quite quickly.

GO THE EXTRA MILE

When frying any meat, a little knob of butter added in halfway through cooking will add fantastic flavour and improve the golden colour you're aiming for. Add it too soon though and it has the chance to burn, turn dark brown and taint the meat.

MOLTEN PLASTIC WON'T HELP ANYONE

Larger cuts of meat, like a whole chicken breast or pork chop, benefit from frying in a hot pan to start, then transferring the same pan to the oven to finish off. Just make sure the pan is ovenproof. Plastic handles are a mistake!

hot smoky pan
rare

medium

well done

sirloin steak with horseradish mash

4 beef sirloin steaks (about 200g per steak)
4 large portabella mushrooms
few sprigs of fresh thyme
2 cloves of garlic
butter
2 tbsp horseradish sauce
1 × classic mash

preheat the oven to 220°C.

rub the steak in seasoned oil, then fry in a very hot frying pan to seal it and give it a golden colour.

scrub clean the mushrooms and place them in an ovenproof dish with a lid.

strip the leaves from the thyme and sprinkle over the mushrooms.

grate the garlic over and dot with small bits of butter. Season well and cover with the lid.

bake in the preheated oven for about 5–6 minutes.

cook the steak to personal preference (see page 84), then leave the meat to rest in a warm place for at least 3 minutes.

beat the horseradish into the hot **classic mash** and serve with the steak and the baked mushrooms. A side order of steamed spinach or green beans is great with this.

    mins

chicken and black pudding with colcannon

4 chicken breasts

head of savoy cabbage

1 onion

black pudding sausage (200g)

1 × classic mash

knob of butter

preheat the oven to 200°C.

rub the chicken breasts in seasoned oil and lay them on a baking tray.

pour over a little water and bake in the preheated oven for about 15–20 minutes.

peel off the leaves of the cabbage and remove the tough centre stalk. Finely shred the cabbage with a knife.

dice the onion and fry it with a dash of oil in a saucepan, then add the cabbage and cook for a few minutes.

slice the black pudding into rounds (after removing the plastic casing!). Fry in a hot pan for a few minutes so it gains a crisp outside but is still soft inside.

beat the cooked cabbage (which should still be nice and green) into the hot **classic mash** and add a little more butter.

balance the cooked chicken and black pudding on top of the colcannon to serve.

skewered paprika chicken with sweet potato mash and crispy salad

couple of sweet potatoes
4 chicken breasts
shot of oil
1 lemon
smoked paprika
pinch of salt
1 × classic mash made using half regular potatoes and half sweet potatoes
crisp mixed-leaf salad

preheat the grill to very hot.

cut any fatty bits out of the chicken.

slice the chicken breast into thin strips.

soak the chicken in the oil, the juice from the lemon, a sprinkle of smoked paprika and a pinch of salt.

thread the strips of chicken onto water-soaked wooden skewers – enough for at least a couple each.

grill the skewers under the preheated grill – or, even better, on a BBQ – to char the outside but leave the inside succulent.

serve the skewers straight from the grill with the sweet potato mash and salad tossed in your chosen dressing.

££ ☺ ×4 ◑ mins

fishy fishy fishy

The know-how when it comes to fresh fish is a valuable addition to any cook's repertoire. Buying whole fish can save you money and you'll also have a better indication of quality. You'll get two fillets from a round fish and this is usually a big portion for one or enough for two lighter meals.

1 **FRESHNESS COUNTS**
When buying whole fish there are a few key points to watch out for:

There shouldn't be any fishy smell. Yes, it should smell a little of the sea or fresh water, but it should not have that pungent pong that many wrongly associate with fish.

Flesh on the fish should be firm. If it gives way under a little pressure it indicates that the fish is a bit older than it should be.

The scales should still be attached to the body and not beginning to flake away.

The gills (flaps on the side of the head) ought to be bright red. You may need to lift these to check inside.

Based on the fact that the fishmonger has already scaled and gutted the slippery critter for you:

2 Remove any excess scales by rubbing the back of the knife along its body from the tail to the head. Wipe these up with a cold damp cloth, to avoid getting too messy. Never use hot water to clean up scales – it more or less turns them to glue!

3 Snip off the fins from the side and back of the fish.

4 Cut into the fish, through to the backbone, just behind its head. The closer you get, the less good fish you waste.

5 Turn the knife towards the tail and run it along the body right to the tail to remove one of the fillets. Feel the knife scraping along the backbone – again, this avoids leaving flesh on the bone. Flip the fish over and repeat the process on the other side to leave just the skeleton.

6 Run the knife under the ribcage of each fillet to remove all of the little bones in one clean slice. Trim any excess fatty flesh away to tidy up the fillet.

7 Slide your finger gently along the centre of the fillet and you'll feel some very small bones. Pluck these out with a pair of tweezers to leave you fish fillets ready for cooking (pin-boning).

8 Your fish is now ready to fry!!!

9 Fry the fish, skin side down, in a hot pan with half oil and half butter. Season the flesh of the fish as it cooks and finish in the pan with a squeeze of lemon juice.

1
2
3
4
5
6
7
8
9

baked trout on celeriac and fennel mash with roasted roots

2 carrots
2 parsnips
4 shallots
olive oil
1 celeriac
1 head of fennel
2 whole trout
1 lemon
1 × classic mash (substitute celeriac and fennel for half the potato)

preheat the oven to 200°C.

peel the carrots, parsnips and shallots.

halve the shallots and cut the carrots and parsnips into finger-sized chunks.

rub them all in a little seasoned olive oil and roast on a tray in the oven for about half an hour.

cut away the skin from the celeriac and chop into chunks the same size as the potatoes for the mash.

remove the root then slice the fennel.

substitute fennel and celeriac for half of the potato in the **classic mash** and continue as per mash instructions.

fillet, pin-bone and trim the fish into portions and bung them on a baking tray. See page 90 for more details.

squeeze over the juice of a lemon and season with salt and pepper.

bake in the preheated oven for the last 8–10 minutes of the roasted vegetable cooking time, until just cooked.

serve the fish immediately with the roasted veg and the creamy celeriac and fennel mash.

    mins

pan-fried cod on garlic and basil mash, with roasted vine tomatoes

cherry tomatoes on the vine (about 24)

shot of olive oil

4 portions of cod (skin on)

1 × classic mash cooked with 3 whole peeled cloves of garlic

handful of fresh basil

flavoured butter (optional)

preheat the oven to 200°C.

cut the vines into portions with about 5–6 tomatoes on each.

lay them on a baking tray, drizzle with oil, season with salt and pepper and roast in the preheated oven until they just begin to burst.

dust the skin of the cod with seasoned flour and fry skin side down in hot oil with a knob of butter, until golden and crisp. Turn over for the last minute or so to complete the cooking.

mash the garlic into the potatoes when they are cooked.

chop the basil fairly roughly with a sharp knife so as not to bruise the leaves and beat into the prepared hot **classic mash**.

serve with some flavoured butter if you have any in the fridge.

flavoured butter

If you're ever left with half a pack of fresh herbs without a home, or you see some on special offer, why not create a flavoured butter?

soften some butter slightly in a microwave and finely chop any herbs you have.

mix them together and spoon the butter onto a stretch of cling film.

roll into a sausage shape and store in the fridge for up to two weeks.

add a slice to finish sauces, enrich soups or garnish steaks and fish.

(Try using crushed garlic, chilli flakes, citrus zest or toasted spices instead of fresh herbs too.)

If it's buckets of flavour and sumptuous meat you're after, then these next few pages are for you.

We reveal the secrets of some awesome dishes with such deep, rich and satisfying flavours that you won't believe how straightforward they are.

stews

You'll only spend a handful of minutes in the kitchen, after which you can just love it and leave it to do its thing – simmering and bubbling away, becoming tastier by the minute while you chill out and do... well, whatever it is you do to chill out. No baby-sitting required!

It's the cheaper cuts of meat that work best here! But they'll need slow, gentle cooking to tenderise the meat and release their magic into the dish. Dinner will be ready when you are – for once you've got the control. If you want to delay mealtime until the decisive moment of that must-see soap, then it can wait. Another 20 minutes in the oven will only do good!

This chapter also suggests a selection of appetising side acts to support the main star of the meal. Whether it's rice, couscous, pastry or dumplings, we'll cover the key points to make sure you nail it every time.

And remember, keep an eye on our website at www.sortedfood.com for more great recipes.

& pies

best cuts of meat

These are popular choices for 'slow cooking'.

They have most flavour as they've been worked hard by the animal but need plenty of time to cook.

beef and Guinness® stew with horseradish dumplings

2 large onions

3 carrots

3 sticks of celery

double shot of vegetable oil

1 heaped tbsp tomato purée

1 tbsp plain flour

1 can of Guinness® beer (440ml)

beef stock (250ml)

diced shin of beef (1kg)

2 bay leaves

sprig of fresh thyme

3 cloves of garlic

dumpling ingredients:

beef suet (150g)

self-raising flour (150g)

salt and freshly ground black pepper

2 tbsp horseradish sauce

water to bind

preheat the oven to 160°C.

hack up the peeled onions, carrots and celery into thumb-sized pieces.

dump into a large casserole pan with the oil and fry over high heat, allowing the veg to brown and scraping up the browned bits from the bottom of the pan as you go.

add the tomato purée and flour once the vegetables are coloured, stirring until the flour is all mixed in.

pour the Guinness® into the casserole, followed by the beef stock.

bring up to a gentle simmer and add the beef to the casserole. Season with salt and pepper and add the bay leaves, thyme and garlic.

cover the casserole with a lid and place in the preheated oven to cook for 2–3 hours, checking occasionally to stir and make sure the side isn't catching and burning.

place the suet in a bowl and sift in the flour. Using one clean hand, mix the suet and flour well, then season with salt, freshly ground black pepper and horseradish sauce.

create a 'well' in the centre of the mixture and add water a bit at a time. Mix with your hands until you get a firm dough that comes away cleanly from the sides of the bowl.

turn out the dough onto a clean board and sprinkle over some flour.

roll the dough out into a sausage shape, then form into 10 golf ball sized dumplings (they'll double in size when cooking). Carefully drop the dumplings into the stew for the last half an hour of cooking.

serve the dumplings and beef stew in large bowls with fresh veg. You'll know when the beef's done because it will almost fall apart when touched. The dumplings should be light and fluffy.

couscous ingredients:

2 mugs of couscous
fistful of sultanas
1 tsp salt
1 tsp turmeric
couple of spring onions
2 mugs of boiling water
glug of olive oil
fistful of fresh coriander

lamb and apricot tagine with spiced couscous

Tagine might sound exotic... but honestly, it's just a fancy name for a rich and aromatic stew that originates from North African countries. It's another brilliant way of using tougher and cheaper cuts of meat and transforming them into succulent mouth-watering meals. The lamb works particularly well with the sweetness of the apricots, cinnamon and almonds in our twist on this classic Moroccan dish.

2 large onions
shot of olive oil
1 tbsp ground cumin
1 tbsp ground coriander
1 tbsp ground cinnamon
3 cloves of garlic
lamb leg or shoulder, boned (1kg)
lamb or veg stock (400ml)
2 tbsp honey
juice of a small lemon
5 or 6 tomatoes
2 fistfuls of dried apricots
fistful of flaked almonds
1 tbsp salt and ground black pepper

preheat the oven to 160°C.

peel and slice the onions, then fry them in the oil in an ovenproof saucepan for 5 minutes.

spoon the dried spices, salt and pepper into the onions with the peeled and crushed garlic and cook for a minute.

tip the trimmed and diced lamb into the pan and cover with the stock, adding the honey and lemon juice.

hack up the tomatoes and put all of the flesh, seeds and juice in the pan.

bring the mixture to a gentle simmer, cover with a lid and place it into the preheated oven for an hour.

add the apricots and stir the tagine well. Return to the oven for another 30 minutes without the lid.

place the couscous in a bowl with the sultanas, salt and turmeric, and throw in some finely sliced spring onions.

pour the boiling water into the couscous, stir then cover the bowl with a lid for 3 minutes.

toast the almonds in a dry pan until golden all over and garnish the tagine with them.

fluff up the couscous with a fork and mix in the olive oil and finely chopped fresh coriander.

serve the tagine with the couscous.

££ ×4 2 hrs

"taste the difference luvvies. or i'll 'ave you!!"

Tom
(aka Granny Barnes)

beef rendang and aromatic rice

Stewing beef is one of the most popular cuts of meat for slow-cooking methods. This rendang is not as commonly found in the UK as perhaps beef in ale or beef in red wine, and that's what **SORTED** loves about it. Something a little bit different and exciting but using the same methods and techniques. This tasty Indonesian dish steals the show every time!

1 onion

thumb-sized piece of ginger

3 cloves of garlic

2 red chillies

stick of lemon grass

1 lime

1 tsp cinnamon

1 tsp turmeric

1 tsp salt

stewing beef (750g)

shot of vegetable oil

tin of coconut milk (400ml)

mug of desiccated coconut

aromatic rice ingredients:

basmati rice (300g)

5 cardamom pods

cinnamon stick

1 tsp salt

handful of fresh coriander

preheat the oven to 160°C.

peel the onion, ginger and garlic and chop roughly.

throw them into a blender with the chillies, lemon grass, lime zest, spices and salt.

loosen the paste up with the lime juice and a splash of water if needed.

slice the beef into strips and fry in the oil in an ovenproof pan for a couple of minutes to colour.

spoon in the aromatic paste and fry for another 2 minutes, then pour in the coconut milk.

toast the desiccated coconut in a dry pan until golden and tip into the rendang mix.

place the pan in the preheated oven and cook for an hour with the lid on and an additional half an hour without the lid, until most of the liquid has evaporated and what is left is a dark and rich curry-style dish.

wash the rice in the meantime to remove any excess starch and leave to drain.

with 25 minutes to go...

transfer the rice to a pan with the cardamom pods, cinnamon stick, 750ml of water and salt, then bring to the boil.

simmer until most of the water has been absorbed, then place on a lid and after about 30 seconds remove the pan from the heat.

leave the rice to rest for 10 minutes or so, and you'll end up with perfectly cooked and fluffy grains.

chop up the fresh coriander and mix through the rice as you serve it with the beef rendang.

££ ×4 2 hrs

chicken and leek pie

Variations of similar pies can be found scattered across pub menus up and down the country – with good reason. They taste great. But none is as satisfying as when you make the pie yourself. The beauty of it is that once you have the know-how you can make the fillings to your pies as humble or as sophisticated as you like. Some might argue that life's too short to make your own pastry, so for this recipe we've cheated and used off-the-shelf pastry.

bottle of cider (500ml)
2 carrots
2 bay leaves
3 leeks
4 chicken breasts, sinew and fat removed
butter (50g)
plain flour (50g)
milk (200ml)
1 tsp wholegrain mustard
packet of ready-rolled puff pastry
1 egg

pour the cider into a saucepan and bring to the boil.

peel and slice the carrots, add them to the cider with the bay leaves and simmer for 5 minutes.

halve the leeks lengthways and slice fairly thinly, then dump them into a colander and wash well to get rid of any mud or grit.

add the washed leeks to the simmering cider with the whole chicken breasts and cover with a lid. Simmer for about 15 minutes.

strain the contents of the pan through a sieve, collecting all the liquid in a bowl.

tear the cooked chicken into strips when it's cool enough to handle.

melt the butter in the now empty pan and stir in the flour. Add the strained liquid a bit at a time over a high heat, stirring continuously until a smooth paste forms. Add as much milk as you need to make a sauce the consistency of custard.

tip the cooked chicken, carrots and leeks into the sauce, mix in the mustard and season well with salt and pepper. Pour everything into an ovenproof dish.

roll out the puff pastry on a lightly floured surface to the thickness of a pound coin.

brush the edges of the pie dish with milk or beaten egg, then drape the rolled pastry over.

press the edges against the dish to stick, then cut away any excess. Brush over all the pastry with beaten egg. This makes the pastry go golden brown and look the business.

poke a hole in the pastry lid to let the steam out when cooking.

bake the pie at 180°C for 25–30 minutes then serve with fresh steaming vegetables and some mashed spuds.

now the food's
under control,

put your feet up and
whack on your fav film!

Jamie

light and fragrant fish stew

A fantastic dish, which by definition is a stew, although one that is relatively quick to make. Yes, it needs gentle cooking like the others but for not nearly as long and it's done on top of the stove. And this sneaky little tip of using the garlic mayo to thicken the stew gives the dish a unique twist.

few strands of saffron

1 leek

1 head of fennel

shot of olive oil

small new potatoes (500g)

fish stock (600ml)

mixed fish fillets (500g)

zest of half an orange

selection of other seafood – squid, raw king prawns, scallops, mussels, clams (about 250g in total)

bunch of chervil or flat-leaf parsley

mayonnaise ingredients:

1 egg

1 tbsp lemon juice

clove of garlic

mild olive oil (100ml)

make the mayo by cracking the egg into a blender with the lemon juice and crushed garlic clove. Then blitz.

drizzle the oil into the blender slowly while it's spinning (be careful) until you get the consistency of mayonnaise. (You can make the mayo by hand using a whisk but it takes a little longer!) Season and leave the mayo to one side for later.

stick the saffron strands into a cup, pour in a little boiling water and leave the saffron to infuse.

wash and finely slice the leek and fennel, then sweat them off in a pan with the oil, covered with a lid so that they soften without gaining colour, about 3–4 minutes.

scrub the potatoes clean and cut them in half.

pour the fish stock into the fennel and leeks and add the potatoes.

simmer for 10 minutes, until the potatoes are almost cooked.

skin and de-bone the fish (see page 90) and cut it into matchbox-sized pieces.

scatter the orange zest into the pan along with the saffron and the infused water and stir well.

place the fish into the pan and poach, with the liquid just under boiling point, for about 2 minutes, then add in the seafood selection and poach for a further 2–3 minutes.

chop the herbs and mix these in at the last moment.

finish the stew by stirring through some of the garlic mayo. This will thicken the soup and give it a luxurious silky feel. Don't boil the stew after adding the mayo.

adjust the seasoning with salt and pepper and serve with some crusty bread.

It doesn't matter where the biscuit barrel is hidden, we all seem to have developed a sixth sense that tells us exactly where it is, what's in it and how many are there!

Denial merely makes the sugar cramps more acute. Until the last single chocolate chip from the last single chocolate chip cookie is gone you just can't relax, can you? So go on – find the little critter and eat it!

cakes

Why is there so much shame associated with this guilty pleasure? Well, "I made them myself" puts a completely different spin on it (bear with us)... it's one thing entirely if you buy biscuits from the corner shop and scoff them all – that's plain lazy – for couch potatoes only. Instead cooking your own cakes, cookies and tarts takes focus, precision and skill, and you are creating something for your mates and for those elusive moments when you deserve a treat.

Well now we've got that straight let's get cracking. These beauties are actually pretty straightforward to make, with bog-standard cupboard ingredients that will keep for ages.

And remember, keep an eye on our website at www.sortedfood.com for more great recipes.

& tarts

SAMSUNG

baking tips

KEEP YOUR HANDS COOL!

Working with pastry can be a delicate procedure and the dough doesn't really appreciate excessive treatment from hot hands. Limit the time you spend manoeuvring the dough, and run your hands under cold running water then dry them quickly before handling it.

IS IT NEARLY DONE YET?

Every oven will operate in its own way so the cooking times in the recipes are approximate. Always check the cake's done before taking it out. An under-cooked cake will sink in the middle as it cools and be stodgy to eat, while over-cooking will result in a dry sponge that needs a glass of milk to stop you choking on the crumbs. A simple solution is to stick a clean skewer or cocktail stick into the centre of the cake and pull it back out slowly. If it's clean the cake is done, but if any gooey mix can be seen on the skewer give it a little longer.

THE FINISHING TOUCHES

A great cake or cookie can be transformed into a stunning work of art with a little extra attention. Slicing a basic sponge in two and wedging it back together with cream and jam is always a favourite. Or why not try one of these two straightforward icings:

Glacé icing – nothing more than sieved icing sugar slowly bound together with a drop or two of cold water. Try and sex it up with some food colouring or extra liquid flavouring. Then add a tiny bit of water at a time – you'll be surprised how little it needs. Carefully spread it around and leave to set.

Butter icing – beat together twice as much icing sugar as soft butter and stir through whatever takes your fancy. Coffee essence, citrus zest or cocoa powder are brilliant options. Use it like glue to stick sponges together, or ice the top of a cake, or pipe it through a nozzle for a decorative finish.

STORAGE

Since you haven't stuffed these sweet treats with loads of preservatives like the shop-bought equivalent they won't last as long. A major difference between cakes and biscuits is how they deteriorate. Cakes and sponges go stale with age, while biscuits and pastry go soggy. You can keep these for longer by bunging them into an airtight box or tin as soon as they are cool. Besides, once tucked away from sight they might be a bit safer from the greedy mitts of friends and family.

SHINY LOOK

Before baking pastry or bread, brush over the rolled out dough with a little milk or a cracked egg. This egg wash will give the finished product the glossy shine that will make your stuff look pro. This is more important for foods that are topped with pastry than for a pastry tart case.

THE SCIENTIFIC BALANCE

The beauty of working with food is that you can throw flavours together, taste it and adjust to excite your own taste buds. That is until you start baking. Bread, pastry and most desserts will only be guaranteed success if you take care in weighing out the items and follow the method.

sponge mix

softened butter (175g)
caster sugar (175g)
3 eggs
self-raising flour (175g)
drop of vanilla extract

preheat the oven to 180°C.

mix the butter and sugar in a bowl until you have a smooth paste that is light and aerated.

beat in the eggs, one at a time, adding a tablespoon of flour with each one and the vanilla extract with the last egg.

sift in the remaining flour and fold through carefully.

scrape the mix into a round non-stick tin or baking tin lined with greaseproof paper, levelling it off.

bake in the preheated oven for 15–20 minutes, until it's golden brown on top and springs back when gently touched with your finger.

turn out onto a wire rack after cooling in the tin for 10 minutes to cool off completely.

microwaveable syrup sponge

This delight is brilliant because it only takes minutes to cook. Chuck together your cake mix, bung it into a microwave-proof bowl, cover and nuke the hell out of it in the microwave for just long enough to get the custard sorted. It's fantastic baking without the... baking!

1 × sponge mix
1 shot of milk
zest of half a lemon
4 tbsp golden syrup

make the classic mix as before but remember to add the additional milk and lemon zest at the end.

grab a big 3 pint bowl and make sure it's microwaveable.

warm a spoon under hot water and measure out the syrup into the bottom of the bowl.

scrape the cake mix on top.

cover the bowl with a microwaveable plate and put the whole thing in the microwave.

nuke it on full power for 4 minutes then leave it to rest for 2 minutes.

turn out onto a plate and dig in immediately.

coconut and lime drizzle cake

1 × sponge mix

half a tin of coconut milk (200ml)

caster sugar (150g)

2 limes

   mins

make the sponge as in the classic recipe and bake in a 900g loaf tin for 30 minutes (ensure it's a non-stick tin or line it well with baking paper).

pour the coconut milk into a small pan with the sugar and bring to a simmer.

dissolve the sugar and simmer for 5 minutes.

add the lime zest and juice and reduce further until thick and syrupy.

pour the lime drizzle mixture over the cake as soon as it is cooked and removed from the oven, while still in its tin.

leave to cool completely in the tin before turning out.

upside-down pear cake

2 pears

handful of brown sugar

cider (100ml)

1 × sponge mix

   mins

preheat the oven to 180°C.

peel the pears, core them and cut into quarters.

lay them in a deep baking tray.

sprinkle with the brown sugar and splash on the cider.

roast in the preheated oven for 15 minutes while you make the sponge mix.

arrange the partly cooked pears skin side down in the bottom of a cake tin, getting rid of as much liquid as possible.

spoon the sponge mix over the pears.

bake for 25 minutes, until golden on top and cooked through.

cookies

softened butter (170g)
white sugar (130g)
brown sugar (140g)
2 eggs
1 tsp vanilla extract
plain flour (260g)
1 tsp baking powder
pinch of salt

preheat the oven to 175°C.

measure the butter and sugars into a bowl and beat with a spoon for a couple of minutes, until fluffy and light. (Blast in the microwave for a few seconds if the butter is rock hard!)

crack in the eggs and beat well.

drip in the vanilla extract and stir through.

sieve in the remaining dry ingredients and fold the cookie dough together until combined.

add your personalised extra ingredient – see some variations below for inspiration.

spoon a teaspoon of the mix onto a non-stick or lined baking tray and gently flatten.

repeat until all the dough has been used, keeping a 2cm space between the cookies for them to spread.

bake in the preheated oven for 15 minutes. They will still be soft but should be slightly golden around the edges.

leave on the tray for a minute or two before lifting them onto a wire rack to cool completely.

scoff them or store in an airtight container when cold for up to 3 days.

mins | makes 24 cookies

a variety of options:

- **100g of chopped milk chocolate and 100g of chopped hazelnuts**
- **zest of an orange and 100g of dried cranberries**
- **100g of chopped glacé cherries and 100g of toasted almond flakes**
- **handful of chopped stem ginger**
- **handful of fresh blueberries**
- **100g of toasted oats**

dive in, get messy
and make a
masterpiece!

sweet pastry case

plain flour (250g)
pinch of salt
cold butter (125g)
icing sugar (50g)
2 eggs
shot of milk (not always required)

THE DOUGH

Sieve the flour and salt into a bowl.

1. Cut the butter into cubes and rub into the flour with your fingertips, just until the mixture resembles breadcrumbs.
2. Stir through the sugar, then add the eggs. Bind into a dough then knead very lightly for a second or two to remove any cracks. Include the milk if the dough is still cracking. Be careful not to overwork it!
3. Wrap the dough in cling film and chill in the fridge for an hour before using. (It can stay in the fridge like this for up to a week if necessary.)

LINING A PIE OR TART TIN

4. Roll out the chilled dough with a rolling pin on a cold, floured and flat surface until it is the thickness of a pound coin and 5cm larger than your tin to allow for shrinkage as it cooks. Transfer the pastry by rolling it gently around the rolling pin and moving it over the tart tin.
5. Unroll it from the pin, ensuring that the pastry overhangs the edges of the tin all the way round by at least 5cm.
6. Lift the overhanging dough with one hand while pressing carefully into the base and sides of the tin. Do not stretch the pastry or force it at this stage. Leave the overhang on the pastry. Chill the tart tin in the fridge for 15 minutes.

BAKING BLIND

Preheat the oven to 200°C.

7. Prick the base of the pastry tart with a fork and cover with a round of greaseproof paper.
8. Fill with dried baking beans, lentils or rice. These act as a weight to stop the pastry rising. Bake for 15 minutes in the preheated oven, then remove the greaseproof paper and beans and bake for a further 5–10 minutes. Keep the beans for next time.
9. Cut away the pastry overhang with a sharp knife when cool, leaving a perfectly smooth and level finish to your tart case.

1 hr | makes 1 large tart case

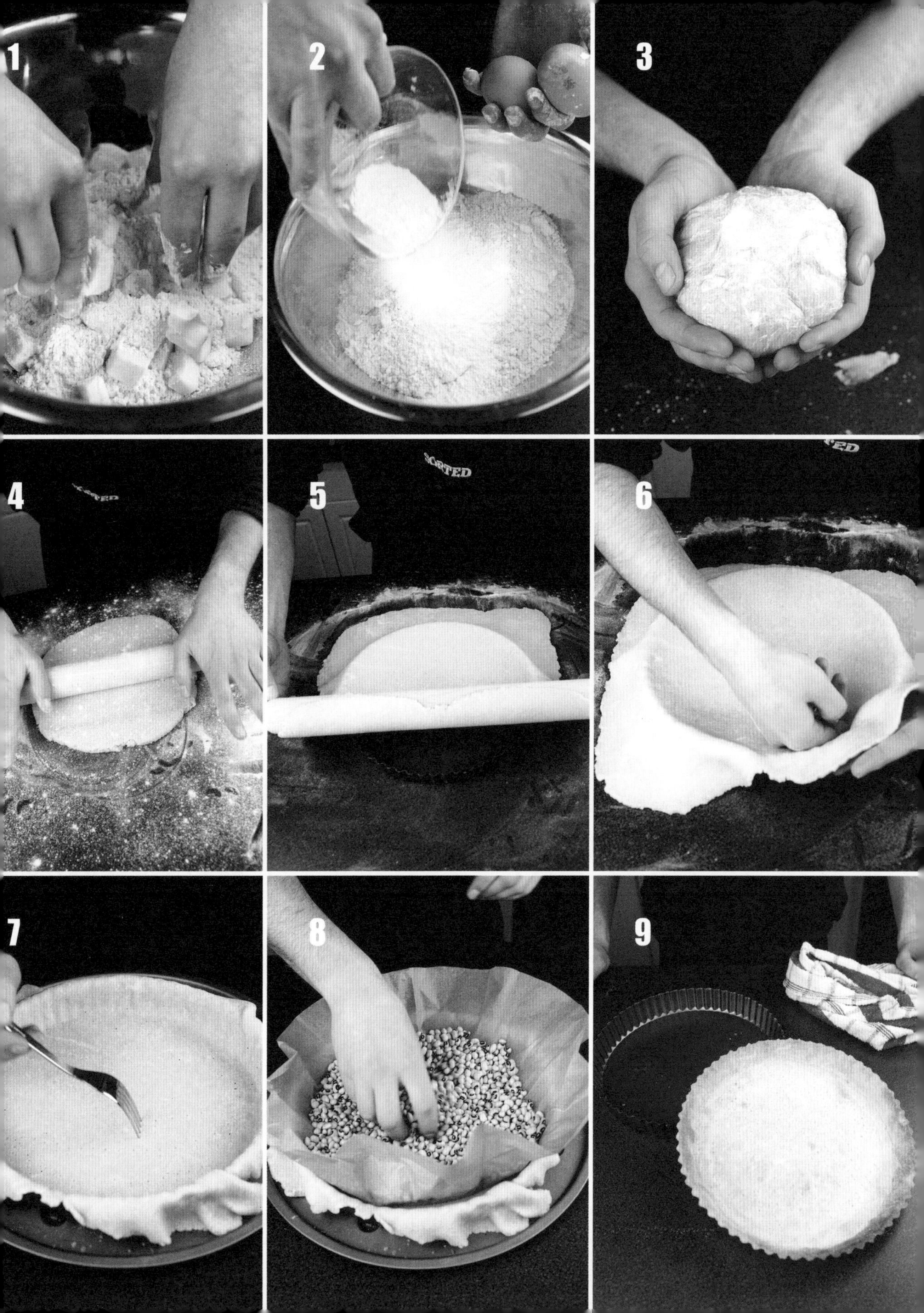
1
2
3
4
5
SORTED
6
7
8
9

fresh fruity tart

double cream (200ml)

½ a vanilla pod or a drop of vanilla extract

fresh custard (100ml)

1 × sweet pastry case

selection of fresh fruit with loads of colour (strawberry, kiwi, peach, purple grapes, mandarin segments)

couple of spoonfuls of apricot jam

icing sugar

whip the cream until you have soft peaks.

scrape out the seeds from the vanilla pod and fold them into the cream with the fresh cold custard, or add the vanilla extract.

spoon the creamy vanilla custard into the pastry case.

prepare all the fruit as neatly as possible and arrange in the pastry case in rows or sections of colour.

melt the jam in a bowl in the microwave, then brush it over the finished tart to give it a shine.

dust with icing sugar and serve – always best eaten at room temperature.

    mins

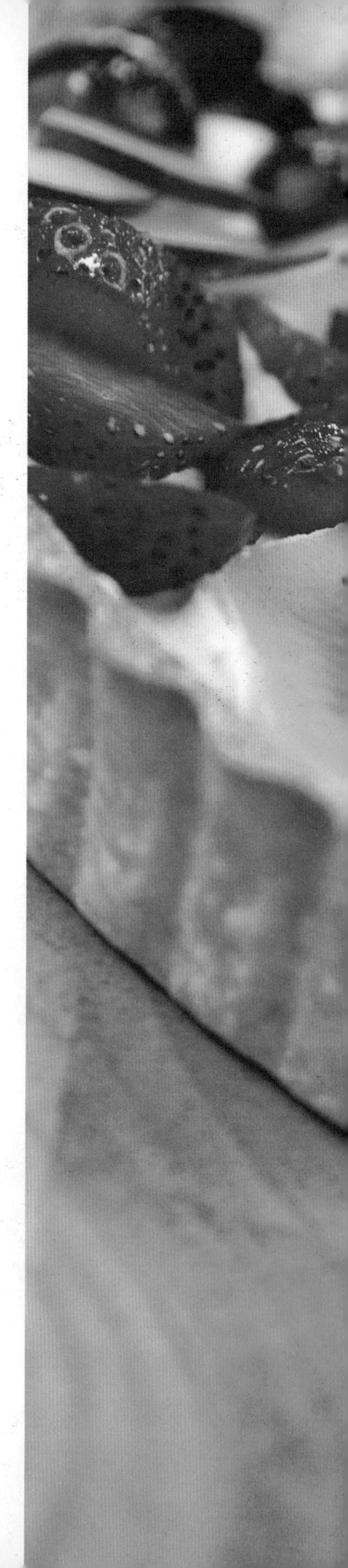

banoffee pie

large tin of condensed milk (397g)

4 × small individual sweet pastry cases

handful of chopped hazelnuts

mug of double cream (200ml)

3–4 bananas

few squares of dark chocolate

place the unopened tin of condensed milk in a saucepan and add water to come halfway up the side of the tin.

bring to the boil and simmer for 2½ hours. Keep topping up the pan with water so that it doesn't boil dry.

leave the tin to cool completely. (Why not make several of these at a time? They keep for months if not opened.)

open the tin to reveal glossy toffee and half-fill your pastry case with it.

toast the hazelnuts in a dry pan until they go golden.

whip the cream until soft peaks form and spread over the toffee.

peel and slice the bananas and arrange them generously on top just before serving.

decorate by grating over some dark chocolate and a sprinkle of the toasted nuts.

chocolate and amaretti tart

plain chocolate (100g)

softened butter (125g)

caster sugar (125g)

3 large eggs

self-raising flour (25g)

ground almonds (125g)

amaretti biscuits (50g)

tin of pitted cherries (400g)

1 × sweet pastry case

handful of flaked almonds

£££ ×8 1.5 hrs

preheat the oven to 150°C.

break up the chocolate and melt in a small heatproof bowl over a pan of simmering water.

beat the butter and sugar in a large bowl until creamy and light.

stir in the eggs one at a time until smooth.

fold in the flour and ground almonds.

crush the amaretti biscuits and carefully add these to the mix with the melted chocolate.

spoon half of the mix into the tart case.

scatter over a handful of the drained cherries and cover with the remainder of the mix.

sprinkle with the almond flakes and bake in the preheated oven for 1 hour.

cool in the tin for 15 minutes before attempting to remove.

Surely the best bit? The nuts! The dogs! The cherry on top!

pudd

It doesn't matter how strong-willed you are and how menacingly that calorie counter haunts you – every once in a while, for one night only, you just have to go the full monty! These are serious crowd pleasers to punctuate the end of a wicked meal, leaving your guests happier than ever. Go on – make 'em weak at the knees!

Most of these pleasure-seeking desserts can be made ahead of time when the kitchen is calm and you can put all your love and attention into crafting them, making any cock-ups on the quiet! The secret is to keep it simple but then do the flamboyant presentation bit to give it the wow factor.

And besides, the proof of the pudding is in the eating! So we guess it would be rude not to, wouldn't it?

And remember, keep an eye on our website at www.sortedfood.com for more great recipes.

Rach

Rach & Beth admire
Alex's dessert,

if not his table manners

Alex
Beth

ice creams

basic mix

double cream (600ml)
large tin of condensed milk (397g)
drop of vanilla essence

whip the cream lightly until it forms soft peaks.

stir through the condensed milk and vanilla essence along with your flavour of choice – some ideas are below.

pour into a suitable container and freeze for a couple of hours.

whisk the mix up now that it is a bit slushy then return to freezer to solidify completely.

leave the ice cream out of the freezer to soften for 10 minutes before serving.

enjoy pure perfection!

chocolate cookie

200g melted dark chocolate
200g crushed chocolate cookies

banana and peanut

2 tbsp crunchy peanut butter
1 mashed up banana

brown bread

yes... that's brown bread!

two fistfuls of toasted breadcrumbs
sprinkle of mixed spice

berry and almond

plenty of crushed berries
handful of toasted almonds

££ ×4 mins + freezing

traditional apple and cinnamon crumble

cooking apples (about 1 kg)

double shot of orange juice

brown sugar (120g)

sprinkle of cinnamon

plain flour (120g)

cold butter (80g)

   mins

preheat the oven to 180°C.

core the apples, then peel and cut into chunks.

place them in a pan with the orange juice, a handful of the sugar and the cinnamon.

stew the fruit for just a few minutes, until the apple chunks begin to soften around the edges.

tip into an ovenproof dish.

sift the flour into a clean bowl and add the diced butter.

rub the two together with your fingertips until it all looks like breadcrumbs.

stir through the rest of the sugar and sprinkle over the half-cooked apples.

bake for about 30 minutes, until golden on top and the apples are beginning to bubble up at the sides.

homemade custard

half a vanilla pod or a drop of vanilla essence

milk (500ml)

6 egg yolks

2 heaped tbsp caster sugar

    mins

scrape the seeds from the pod and add them (or the vanilla essence) to the milk in a pan.

bring to a gentle boil, stirring occasionally.

whisk the egg yolks and sugar in a clean bowl.

pour the boiling milk over the egg yolks while whisking.

return to the pan and stir continuously over a gentle heat until the custard thickens and will coat the back of a spoon. Take care 'cos if you heat it too quickly or for too long you'll end up with sweet scrambled egg – not a good look!

take off of the heat and pass through a sieve to remove any lumps.

chill and serve cold, or re-heat as required in the microwave.

rhubarb and ginger with granola crumble

rhubarb (1kg)

caster sugar (200g)

preserved stem ginger (30g)

bowl of luxury granola cereal

1 orange

   mins

wash the rhubarb and cut into strips the size of your thumb.

stick them in a pan with the sugar and a few drops of water, and cook over a gentle heat for about 10 minutes.

zest the orange and finely dice the stem ginger, then add them to the partially stewed fruit.

lay the granola on an oven tray and warm through in the oven.

assemble the crumbles on individual plates by stacking the cooked rhubarb through a ring and topping with the warm and crisp granola.

serve with ice cream and wow your guests with this easy twist on a crumble-style dessert.

plum and vanilla with flapjack crumble

plums (about 12)

brown sugar (120g)

vanilla pod

butter (100g)

golden syrup (125g)

porridge oats (250g)

    mins

preheat the oven to 180°C.

stone and quarter the plums and stick them in a pan with a handful of the sugar and the split vanilla pod.

splash in a shot or two of water and cook for 3–4 minutes over a gentle heat until the fruit starts to soften.

dump the partly stewed fruit into an ovenproof dish.

melt the butter, syrup and remaining sugar in a pan until the sugar has dissolved.

stir through the porridge oats, then spread over the plums.

bake in the preheated oven for 25 minutes, until golden and gooey.

leave to stand for 10 minutes before serving a whopping great portion with ice cream.

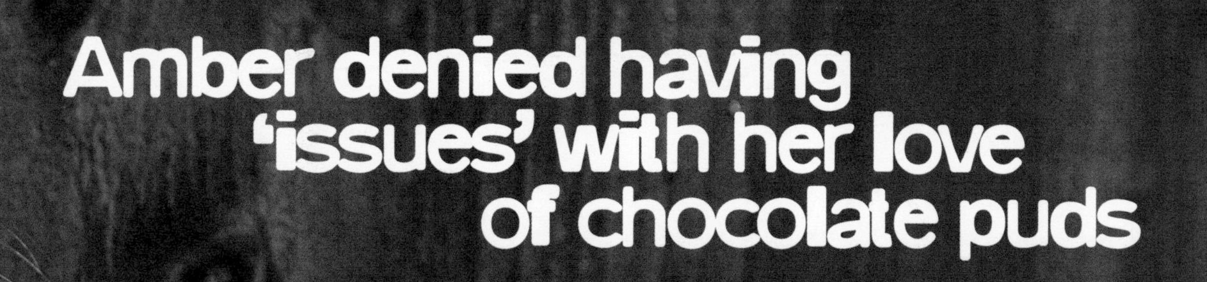
Amber denied having
'issues' with her love
of chocolate puds

meringue base

4 egg whites
caster sugar (120g)
icing sugar (120g)

1 **separate** the egg whites from their yolks and place the whites into a clean bowl.
2 **whisk** them up to stiff peaks.
Measure in the caster sugar and start whisking again until you reach stiff peaks again.
3 **sift** in the icing sugar and carefully fold together.

pavlova or roulade ingredients:

1 × meringue base
double cream (250ml)
2 tbsp icing sugar
drop of vanilla extract
plenty of your favourite vibrant fresh fruit

pavlova

1 **spoon** the meringue made above into a piping bag.
2 **squeeze** it through a star nozzle onto a baking paper lined oven tray to form little individual nests. Bake at 125°C, with a tea towel wedged in the oven door to keep it open slightly and let out any steam, for an hour and a half. These should be dry enough to pick up but still have a slightly chewy centre. Whip up the double cream to stiff peaks and sweeten with icing sugar and a little vanilla.
3 **dollop** it onto the cooled nests and pile on as much neatly prepared fruit as you dare.

roulade

1 **spread** the meringue mix into a thin layer right across a baking paper lined oven tray. Bake at 150°C for 30–35 minutes, until crisp on the outside but chewy in the centre. Remove and allow to fully cool. Place the cooled sheet of meringue on a clean tea towel, making it easier to roll. Whip up the double cream to stiff peaks, sweeten and flavour with a little vanilla before spreading a thin layer over the whole sheet of meringue.
2 **scatter** a variety of fruit over the cream and carefully roll the meringue from one end to the other.
3 **decorate** with a dusting of cocoa powder and perhaps a few toasted nuts.

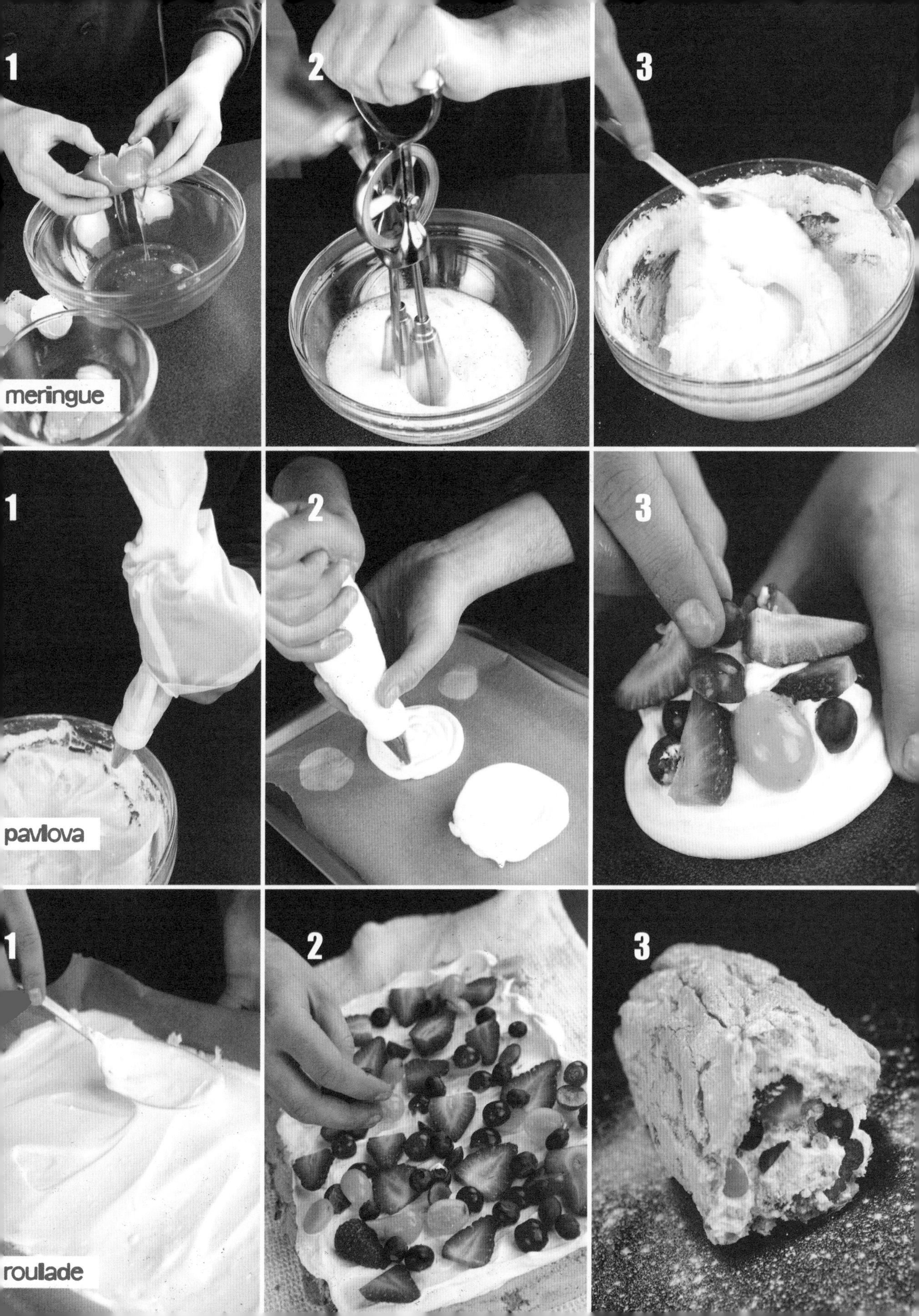
1
2
3
meringue
1
2
3
pavlova
1
2
3
roulade

basic chocolate mousse

chocolate (250g)
milk (100ml)
additional flavour (see below)

double cream (280ml)
3 large egg whites

   mins + chilling

crack the chocolate into small pieces and place in a heatproof bowl with the milk.

heat gently over a pan of simmering water until melted and silky smooth, adding the additional flavour if using any.

leave aside to cool for 10 minutes.

whip the cream to soft but floppy peaks.

whisk the egg whites in another bowl to soft peaks.

fold the cream into the chocolate mixture as carefully as possible, then do the same with the egg whites.

divide into individual glasses, dishes or cups and chill for at least 4 hours.

cappuccino mousse

1 × basic chocolate mousse (using dark chocolate)
3 tsp 'Camp chicory & coffee essence' or 2 tbsp strong black espresso coffee

chocolate orange mousse

1 × basic chocolate mousse (using milk chocolate)
grated zest of 1 large orange

white chocolate and raspberry mousse

1 × basic chocolate mousse (using white chocolate)
small box of fresh raspberries (half of them mashed up)

bunch of fools

You'd be one not to give this simple and tasty pud a go. Fools can look so pro if you take care to layer them up as you go along. But they taste just as good if slopped in a bowl and devoured as a real comforting pud too.

classic fool mix

crème fraîche (150ml)

natural yoghurt (150ml)

2 tbsp icing sugar

additional ingredients (see below)

   mins

beat the crème fraîche and yoghurt together in a large bowl.

sift in the icing sugar to sweeten.

prepare all the additional ingredients as required (details below).

layer into a presentational glass and garnish accordingly.

peach and lemon

tin of peach slices in natural juice

dollop of lemon curd

shortbread biscuits

drain the peaches and chop into small pieces.

stir the lemon curd through the yoghurt mix.

crush the biscuits slightly then build your fool by layering the lemon curd yoghurt with peach pieces and bits of shortbread.

banana and honey

handful of flaked almonds

1 banana

squeeze of runny honey

toast the almonds in a dry pan until they begin to colour and smell like popcorn.

peel and thinly slice the banana.

construct the dessert by squeezing in layers of honey, banana, yoghurt mix and cooled almond flakes.

eton mess

meringue nest
handful of mixed soft red berries
few sprigs of fresh mint

crush the meringue nest to form small pieces.

mash half of the berries and leave the rest whole.

shred the mint leaves as finely as possible and stir through the yoghurt mix.

construct the dessert by combining berries, meringue and yoghurt mix to gain a marbled effect and finish with meringue pieces and whole berries.

iced lemon and ginger torte

packet of ginger nut biscuits (300g)
melted butter (100g)
3 egg whites
double cream (200g)
caster sugar (80g)
5 egg yolks
zest and juice of 3 lemons
fresh berries

blitz the biscuits in a blender or whack them in a plastic bag with a hefty rolling pin.

melt the butter over a gentle heat or in the microwave and combine with the biscuit crumbs.

press down firmly into a large loose-bottomed cake tin and chill.

whisk the egg whites to stiff peaks in a clean bowl.

whip the cream to soft peaks in another bowl.

beat the sugar and egg yolks together in large bowl and add the grated zest and juice.

fold in the egg whites, then the cream, and pour onto the prepared biscuit base.

freeze for at least 4 hours.

warm the edges slightly with the palms of your hands and ease the torte from the tin.

cut a slice and serve with a few fresh berries. Blueberries work a treat.

note: Make this whenever you're bored and have time. It'll keep in the freezer (if wrapped in cling film) for well over a month. Always on hand when you need a flashy pudding at a moments notice!

Help is on hand from our resident drink doctor as we prescribe a dose of wet and wonderful ideas to quench your thirst.

Our smoothies get those early mornings off to an energetic and fruity start, or if you'd rather chill out in the summer months try our refreshing, homemade milkshake or fruit punch.

Our thirst-aider, Billy-boy the Barman, shows how to throw together a range of his speciality punches and 'mocktails' with enough style and flair to become the talking point of any night in with your mates. As ever, these ideas and flavours are only the beginning of what's possible. Why not slip into mixologist mode and see what you can come up with? Cheers!

And remember, keep an eye on our website at www.sortedfood.com for more great drinks and recipes.

thirsty

Gaz

Billy

SORTED mocktails

A traditional mojito will bring a touch of Cuban sunshine to any bar and these two great, alcohol-free, **SORTED** variations never disappoint. They're a perfect balance of sweet cane sugar, bitter lime and refreshing mint, muddled with bucket-loads of ice.

elderflower mojito

2 brown sugar cubes
½ a lime, cut into wedges
5 mint leaves
apple juice (50ml)
elderflower cordial (50ml)
plenty of ice

passion fruit mojito

2 brown sugar cubes
½ a lime, cut into wedges
5 mint leaves
passion fruit juice (100ml)
plenty of ice

stick the sugar cubes, lime wedges and mint into a glass and bash them up with a muddle stick or the end of a wooden spoon.

crush some ice in a blender or in a clean tea towel with a rolling pin.

dump a handful into the glass to half fill it.

pour in the cordial and/or juice and stir the drink well.

serve in a tall glass with fresh lime, a sprig of mint and straw or two.

SORTED zombie

For a silky touch of class with your drinks why not give this one a go? The egg white transforms a regular fruit punch into something that really deserves top slot on any cocktail menu.

½ a lime, cut into wedges
½ a shot of grenadine (12.5ml)
2 shots of pineapple juice (50ml)
2 shots of orange juice (50ml)
½ an egg white (10ml)

measure all of the ingredients into a cocktail shaker.
add a few cubes of ice.
secure on the lid and shake well until a frothy and silky liquid forms.
pour into a glass over more ice.

pineapple tip: As with most cocktails, it's all about the razzle-dazzle presentation. To really get the wow factor why not go to the effort of hollowing out a pineapple? Slice off the top and scoop out the flesh, taking care not to pierce the watertight skin. This is nature's answer to a fancy cocktail glass and raises eyebrows at every occasion. It can be washed out when finished and re-used all night long.

Jamie
Lauren
Jo & Sian

punch party

For the moments when making one drink at a time just won't do the job, simply whip out a punch. It might sound like a wild act of violence but it stems from the word puncheon, the 72 gallon cask in which they used to mix it. But unless you want to bath in it, we're guessing you won't need quite that much.

grab the largest bowl you can find.

pour in the ingredients and juices you love best.

balance the sweet and sour to your own taste by adding in some sugar syrup and/or lime juice.

stir well and ladle in glasses over ice.

pommie apple

equal quantities of apple juice and pomegranate juice
twice as much lemonade

ginger fizz

equal quantities of blueberry juice and cranberry juice
half as much ginger ale

sunny passion

equal quantities of orange juice, grapefruit juice, pineapple juice and passion fruit juice

shakes and smoothies

Milkshakes – a little bit naughty but definitely nice! We could give it our best attempt to convince you that they're a fantastic way to boost your calcium levels and provide you with the necessary dose of vitamin D. But to be frank… it's all a load of tosh. But who cares? They taste superb!

basic shake

cup of milk
2 scoops of ice cream
handful of your additional flavour

slosh the milk into a blender with a double scoop of your chosen ice cream.

tip in your additional flavour (see below), breaking up the items a little if they're large.

whizz for about 30 seconds – long enough to blend in the chunky bits but not so long that you begin to lose the thick and creamy consistency.

pour into a tall glass and garnish with an array of fruit, chocolate shavings, marshmallows or a dusting of cocoa powder.

dive straight in and enjoy.

add some flavour:

honey crunch – vanilla ice cream and a packet of Maltesers.

after-dinner delight – mint choc chip ice cream and a handful of crisp after-dinner mints.

wimbledon common – strawberry ice cream and a few jammy dodgers, topped off with mini marshmallows.

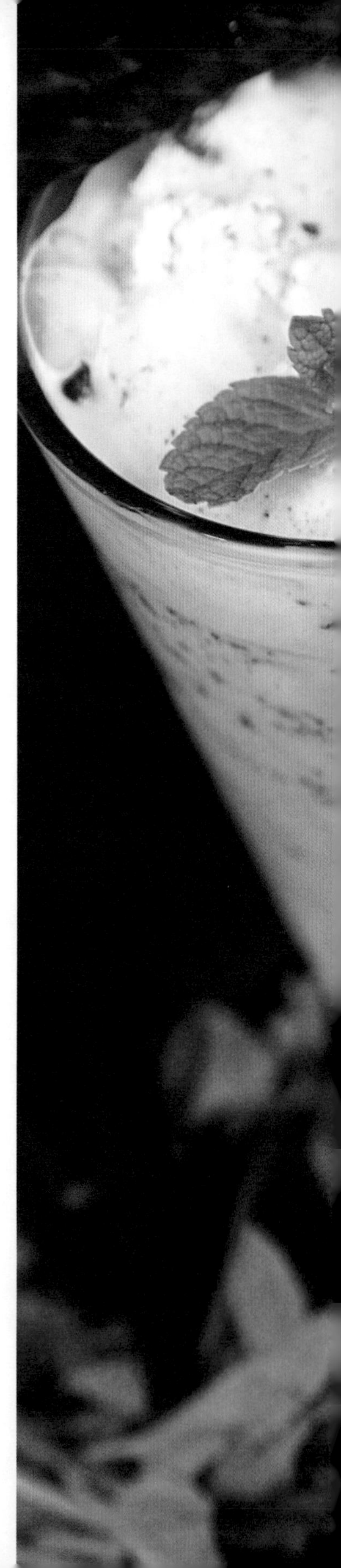

frozen smoothie time

Smoothies are taking the world by storm. They've become the must-have fashion accessory, competing with designer drinks such as mocha cappuccino, skinny latte or café au lait. While some smoothies are dairy-based, we prefer to keep the cows at bay and stick to purely fruity options. Here are some of our favourites. Have a go at these and then experiment with some of your own ideas. Get blitzing!

apple juice (250ml)
your fruit of choice (150g):

1. **strawberry and banana**
2. **pineapple and mango**
3. **melon and mandarin**
4. **apple, pear, blueberry and blackberry**

wash your chosen fruits and peel and prepare them so they are ready to eat.
chop them up into small regular-shaped pieces, ideally the size of a raspberry.
lay them out on a tray and freeze.
scoop them up when individually frozen and store in sandwich bags (about 150g in each) in the freezer until needed.
pour the apple juice into a blender and tip in a bag of fruit that takes your fancy.
blitz for 30 seconds, until your ice-cold fruit smoothie is lump-free and thick.
empty into a glass and slurp through a straw.

tip: You can also buy frozen fruit pre-prepared at some supermarkets. Just add fruit juice, blitz it and Bob's your uncle.

1
2
3
4

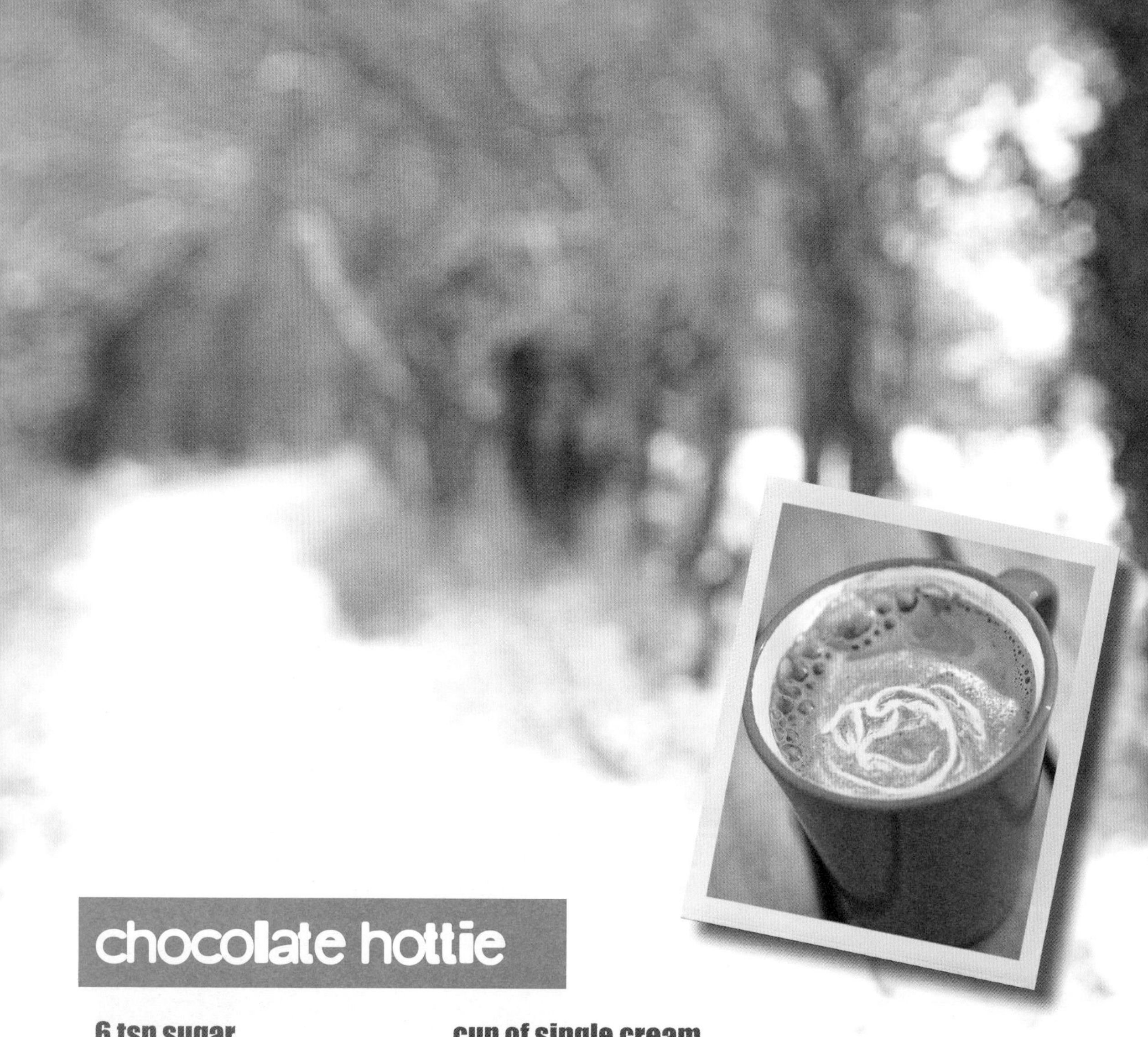

chocolate hottie

- 6 tsp sugar
- 6 tsp unsweetened cocoa powder
- cup of milk
- cup of single cream
- pinch of cinnamon
- ½ tsp vanilla essence
- whipped cream

spoon the sugar and cocoa into the milk and heat in a saucepan until dissolved.

add the cream, cinnamon and vanilla.

heat until almost boiling.

mix well and serve, topped with whipped cream.

index

index cont...

I, J, K, L

M

N, O

P

Q, R

S

T

U, V

W

Z

thanks to...

Barry Taylor

Lora Pike

Tom H

Emily Brennan

Jamie Spafford

Alex Page

Jon Gavaghan

Gary Higgens

Lauren Shoey

Josh Taylor

Adam Wilkinson

Tom Barnes

Nicola Knight

Ben Ebbrell

Tom Moody

Rachel Pike

Mike H

Richard Smith

Josh Reid

Billy Spring

Beth Fox-Fuller

Amber Moore

Steve Lau